D1102865

MY
ANGEL
DIARY
2015

JENNY SMEDLEY

HAY HOUSE

Carlsbad, California • New York City • London • Sydney
Johannesburg • Vancouver • Hong Kong • New Delhi

*Jenny Smedley is the author of many books
that have inspired:*

Ripples
Come Back to Life
Past Life Angels
Past Life Meditation CD
Souls Don't Lie
The Tree That Talked
How to be Happy
Forever Faithful
Supernaturally True
Pets Have Souls Too
Angel Whispers
Soul Angels
Everyday Angels
Pets Are Forever
Angels Please Hear Me
A Year with the Angels
My Angel Diary 2012
An Angel by Your Side
Soul Mates
My Angel Diary 2013
My Dog Diary 2013
My Cat Diary 2013
My Angel Diary 2014
Angelic Healing

Personal Notes

Name _____

Address _____

_____

Phone (home) _____

Phone (work) _____

Phone (mobile) _____

Email _____ _____

In case of emergency please contact:

1.   Name:

     Telephone:

     Relationship:

2.   Name:

     Telephone:

     Relationship:

First published and distributed in the United Kingdom by:
Hay House UK Ltd, Astley House, 33 Notting Hill Gate, London W11 3JQ
Tel: +44 (0)20 3675 2450; Fax: +44 (0)20 3675 2451; www.hayhouse.co.uk

Published and distributed in the United States of America by:
Hay House Inc., PO Box 5100, Carlsbad, CA 92018-5100
Tel: (1) 760 431 7695 or (800) 654 5126
Fax: (1) 760 431 6948 or (800) 650 5115; www.hayhouse.com

Published and distributed in Australia by:
Hay House Australia Ltd, 18/36 Ralph St, Alexandria NSW 2015
Tel: (61) 2 9669 4299; Fax: (61) 2 9669 4144; www.hayhouse.com.au

Published and distributed in the Republic of South Africa by:
Hay House SA (Pty) Ltd, PO Box 990, Witkoppen 2068
Tel/Fax: (27) 11 467 8904; www.hayhouse.co.za

Published and distributed in India by:
Hay House Publishers India, Muskaan Complex, Plot No.3, B-2,
Vasant Kunj, New Delhi 110 070
Tel: (91) 11 4176 1620; Fax: (91) 11 4176 1630; www.hayhouse.co.in

Distributed in Canada by:
Raincoast Books, 2440 Viking Way, Richmond, B.C. V6V 1N2
Tel: (1) 604 448 7100; Fax: (1) 604 270 7161; www.raincoast.com

Text © Jenny Smedley, 2014

The moral rights of the author have been asserted.
All rights reserved. No part of this book may be reproduced by any mechanical, photographic or electronic process, or in the form of a phonographic recording; nor may it be stored in a retrieval system, transmitted or otherwise be copied for public or private use, other than for 'fair use' as brief quotations embodied in articles and reviews, without prior written permission of the publisher. Neither the author nor the publisher can be held responsible for any material on third party websites.

A catalogue record for this book is available from the British Library.

ISBN: 978-1-78180-467-4

Interior images: p.21 © Bruce Rolff/shutterstock

Printed and bound by CPI Group (UK) Ltd, Croydon, CR0 4YY

Contents

Dark Forces

The last part of 2013 and the first part of 2014 were very interesting for me, angelically speaking. Life is a learning curve for all of us, and it never fails to amaze me how steep this curve can get sometimes. I learned many things, some of them repeats of what I thought I'd learned before! Angels must get really fed up with us humans sometimes – well you'd think so, but their patience, it seems, is endless. I also learned that angels of light and energy sometimes have to deal with dark energy/beings. A dear friend of mine was in big trouble and she asked me for help. She thought her problem was just another story of a 'neighbour from hell', but it turned out her trouble was much more serious than that. I have withheld her name for the sake of privacy. This is what she said:

'Our new neighbours were reported to the local Planning Department and decided that we were responsible. Nothing would convince them otherwise. We knew that the woman who lived there was into some spooky stuff, and believed that she had nightly visits from aliens.

'Things turned really bad when we fell out over her music, which could be heard in every corner of our house. We knew she performed ceremonies to gain greater power, and she would make extraordinary sounds while prowling around the garden in a long, black, hooded robe. At first I thought I was seeing a dead monk's ghost, as the robe created the appearance of floating. What with that and the weird hissing sounds she was making, we started to wonder just what she was trying to connect with.

'Strange lights were seen coming from her house – a red one, flashing colours and bright white ones. Other people started to talk – about drugs, about the lights, about the odd strangers seen coming and going late at night – and also commented on the welfare of her two young sons. Inevitably some well-meaning soul reported it all to the police, and of course we were blamed again. She became obsessed, and blamed us for everything that went wrong in her life. She called the police and claimed that I'd broken into her house, fabricating evidence of damage I'd supposedly done. I was cautioned and taken to a police station. My husband and children were terrified. It seemed possible that I could end up in prison.

'Thankfully the police didn't believe her story, but the very fact that she'd actually tried to get me imprisoned and destroy my life was horrifying. The terrors got worse at night, because somehow she'd enter our house after dark in a smoky form.

*One night my husband woke up to find her shape rising up at
him from beside our bed. We thought we were under psychic
attack, and that's when I decided we needed help.'*

My work doesn't allow much time for me to help
people individually, but this was a friend of many years,
albeit one that I hadn't seen for some time, so I had to
try. I have no personal experience of demon possessions
or releases, so it would have been dangerous for me
to attempt anything personally, but still I was able to
see/feel enough that I knew something dramatic and
unusual – and likely dangerous – was going on. The
sensation was so strong that, even remotely, I could feel
the depth of the neighbour's hatred.

In the first instance I connected with my angels to
ask what I should do. With the usual series of angel
'coincidences', they put me back in touch with someone
I'd known years previously who could remove whatever
evil was stalking my friend. This lady, whom I will call
Grace, told me that the power was building, and that
unless my friend got out of the location, she and her
family would be in real danger.

Every day my friend and her family stayed indoors,
too scared to venture into the garden. If they were seen
or heard by the neighbour, it would trigger retaliation.
She once followed them down the road, cackling like a

maniac. They went away several times, just to escape, but it started to look as though they were trapped unless they spent all their savings (and more) and fled.

'Suddenly peace broke out. We couldn't understand it, but Jenny rang to say that 'intervention' had taken place – but that it might be temporary and we must leave immediately. We followed Jenny's advice, and it worked! Someone new fell in love with the house and agreed to take over the 120-year lease. We were assured that whatever it was would never affect them, so that was okay.'

My contact Grace had carried out a ceremony designed to make the darkness leave. It left my friend's neighbour, but then arrived at Grace's house! It threw her backwards into a chair and then floated at ceiling level – a black cloud, writhing around. Her husband held up two pieces of cutlery in the shape of a cross, and threw sea salt at the shape to make it dissolve, and gradually vanish. But, there was always the chance my friend's neighbour might invite it back. We never knew whether she'd conjured it deliberately or got sucked in by it, but she would have been very puzzled by the loss of power.

Needless to say the location of my friend's new home is a secret. If they were ever found, it could all start again...

Light Energy

During the writing of this book, Tony (my husband) and I moved house. Fifteen years ago we'd started living in Somerset, which we loved. People who know me know the story of the way we found our lovely home there, and it was a huge wrench to leave it, but we'd come to miss our family, especially our granddaughter, and now our son and his wife were expecting twins so there would be even more to miss! The move was traumatic in all the usual ways, and some unusual ones.

As well as the normal frustrations, such as the speed of solicitors, awkwardness of the people in the 'chain', arranging removal quotes and changes of address, the temporary lack of internet, management of workloads and so on, we had something else on our minds. Or really, I did. Tony is very sanguine about most things, and I do the panicking for both of us. Some seven years ago, Tony suffered a serious illness that required major surgery. He seemed to have made a total recovery and was checked every year for five years, at which point his surgeon suggested he continue the tests for another five years. Having banked on Tony getting the all clear after five years I was distraught, but once the suggestion of further tests had been made we felt we had to agree.

There was no opportunity to have the test at the time as we had moved into a holiday cottage for three weeks between leaving our old home and moving into our new one (remember I mentioned the awkwardness of the chain!). During the second week we were starting to go a little mad with cabin fever when my angel led me to one particular beech tree in the garden. This tree energized me, calmed me and helped me be patient, and it was a wonderful friend. I was also told that it was going to go on to help the owner of the cottage who had suffered serious breast cancer. Luckily I was able to find a way to tell her that didn't have her thinking I was nuts, and hopefully that tree has now helped her back to full health.

So, Tony was overdue a test the week we finally moved. We signed on with a new GP and Tony asked for a test. The doctor then told us that there was no need to continue with the tests unless Tony needed reassurance. Well, as I already said, Tony doesn't worry like I do. The doctor agreed that after five years of totally negative tests we should draw a line under his illness and get on with our lives. This was great news!

A couple of nights later I slipped out of bed to use the bathroom, and as I got back into bed something very odd happened. I looked back to the bathroom and it lit up with a bright, almost fluorescent green light for three or four seconds. I thought, *did I really see that?* Immediately it lit up again for another few seconds. I got out of bed and looked out of the window, but there are only fields behind the house. I fell asleep again, puzzled. The same night, Tony had a strange dream (or was it a dream?) in which he heard a loud drumming noise and floated up off the bed. When the noise stopped, he fell back down. I gave these things some thought and asked my angel what they meant. Green lights – what else do they mean but 'all clear'? This was a tremendous experience to have, because there was no 'logical' explanation for it. It's not often that anyone gets such amazing and incontrovertible proof of a 'higher power'. And Tony had obviously had something lifted off him, making him 'light-hearted'. Once again my angels had brought me answers to questions I didn't even know I was asking.

Happy Home

Our new house drew us to it. I saw it on the internet, and the pull was there even though we had already made an offer on another, more 'prestigious', house. We were torn between the two, because it did seem like the first one was a great bargain, but after consulting with my angels we decided to go for the more modest second house. It turned out that the first one had a 'tie' on it, and we would have wasted months on a wild goose chase had we proceeded with it. Not only that, but when we added them up (my angels always use numerology to send me messages), the date of our exchange of contracts, the date of completion on our sale, the date of completion on the purchase of the new house, all of the numbers in the address of the new house, each and every one added up to the number 1 (new beginnings) or number 9 (endings). I will also tell you that the name 'Hangman' appears in the address, and whilst some might find this a little spooky, take a look at the meaning of the Hanged Man card in tarot. It totally describes everything one would be going through when deciding to move, right up to finding a new home and dealing with all the complications therein. This symbol was the final proof if ever we needed it that this was our rightful new home.

The Hanged Man generally shows that you're at a crossroads – one that requires a simple 'yes' or 'no'. You might know what you want to do, but find the right path difficult to choose. Just stop and see if you need to let go of something in order to proceed.

Work-wise, things will change and what you thought you *had* to continue with, even if it no longer sits easily with you, or that you were too afraid to let go of, will let *you* go.

Money might be tight, but have faith and a giving heart, and things will improve very soon.

With health – something you fear is wrong turns out not to be the case, and in time you'll be given evidence that you are in control and don't need to worry.

All of these things have happened, exactly…

And, about those twins I mentioned. We had feared that delays in our move would mean we'd miss the big event (twins' births are notoriously difficult to predict), but they waited for us, appearing a couple of weeks after our move.

Learn to Let Go

This will be a year of big decisions for many people and, as in my case, I think they will involve letting go of something in order to achieve something else. With this in mind, I've developed a meditation specifically to help you to let something go.

As usual, make sure you're comfortable and relaxed, breathe regularly, close your eyes and just take a few minutes to welcome your angel to join you, and to feel the love and protection this brings.

Now, in your mind's eye, picture a horizon in front of you. It can be any sort you prefer, but beauty is a good place to start, so why not make it a sunrise, with the sun just peeping above the edge of the world. Now visualize a bubble rise out of the sun, twinkling with rolling colours, like oil on water. This bubble will help you let go of something you are finding difficult to release. This is because we all think and talk of letting go as a 'sacrifice' and humans do not like making sacrifices! Better to imagine the words 'letting go' and 'insert' them into the bubble. See how the object you need to release is welcomed into the bubble and becomes part of it, and that the object you've let go actually enhances the colours that roil over the surface of the bubble? This is a good thing you did, it didn't hurt and soon something new will take its place in your heart and mind. Now visualize the bubble floating up and up, leaving the sun behind and rising into the clouds above. It is free!

Keep this thought in mind as you come back to the world. Realize that your angel is smiling at you, happy and pleased that you've done the right thing to make your life better. You've shown trust and faith, and will be rewarded. Stay still for as long as you like after this meditation. You deserve a rest. Give yourself a break.

One way to make these vibrations more potent and prepare yourself for the changes ahead is to create 'echoes' throughout your day. You don't have to give up all your worldly possessions, but just give to a Big Issue salesperson, or buy someone a cake as a treat, hold open a door or give a little of your precious time to someone who just needs to talk. All these acts will create ripples and empower you more.

Join Forces

This year will be an '8', so as well as the decision-making atmosphere I mentioned earlier, 2015 also represents the coming together of two worlds – that of man and that of animals. This is the year when we really do need to get close to animals as much as we can. Those that already do will tell you how their energy heals and revitalizes, and they more than give back what we give them. Angels are very close to children, but they are also very close to animals, which is why I've chosen to feature one in every week of this diary.

Throughout time, man and animals have been inextricably linked, their fates entwined, and yet man consistently forgets this and treats animals as objects for his use and pleasure. It's hard to believe that there are still people out there who draw pleasure from hunting animals for sport, killing them for fun and treating them cruelly for kicks. I can tell you though, that the last laugh will be on them, because people of this nature will *never* be able to connect with their angels, and will never know the help that would have been available to them if they could.

So, even if you're not a real animal lover, think about these things, look differently upon our animal brothers and understand that not only are we all in this together, but that animals can heal you, help you connect to angels, be a friend and support to you, and ultimately guide you spiritually towards a better future. If you are an animal lover already, then see what more you can do to help them. When you visit an animal shelter for instance, remember that the cute babies will quickly find homes, and once they do, they will soon mature and not be so cute any more. With this in mind, why not choose to help an elderly pet, one who has never done anything wrong and yet has ended up alone and frightened in their last years. It's easy for me because I have an affinity with old dogs, and always have had. Just look into their eyes as they ask, 'What's happened to me?' 'What did I do wrong?' 'Where has my home, my pack, my master, gone?' 'Why am I here alone and scared?', and you'll still see trust and faith there in those eyes. How can you resist, especially if you understand that this animal might help you connect more closely to your angels?

Another two worlds coming together in this year are those of science and spirituality. Watch out for news items showing that the more scientists learn, the closer they are to understanding Universal power and the undoubted benefits of becoming a spiritual being. Links to the examples below are listed in the Resources (*see p.232*). For instance, a study published online by *JAMA Psychiatry* has shown actual physical beneficial brain changes are created in those who consider religious or spiritual beliefs to be high on their list of priorities. Such people even seem to have a form of protection against depression.

A recent issue of *Psychological Science* included a report from researchers at the National Society for Education in Art and Design (NSEAD) and The Wharton School, which proposed that people who meditate are much better at making the right decisions than those who don't. Not long ago meditation was looked upon as being very 'woo woo' by scientists and doctors, but now it's a legitimate tool for the mind.

University of London physicist David Bohm has published a report that appears to include proof of the long-held spiritual belief that we can change or create our reality.

There are many ways that science, in its relentless search for facts, has actually uncovered evidence that there is so much more out there than the material world we take for granted.

So, how can you use angels to bring these two worlds even closer? Simply by looking further than your eyes can take you. The more you accept messages and signs from your angels, the more messages and signs you will receive. I know it's very hard for some people to get going with this, and I get countless letters from people saying they just cannot hear anything from their angels, along with the countless number from people who can. One thing is clear – that it just takes one very small sign, and a giant leap of faith. When people are low and depressed, they simply don't believe that anything good can happen to them, and when it does – even if it's something very small – their logic jumps in instead of their faith, and the sign gets ignored, or denied. For those people, as you read this diary and the stories within, just stop in your daily life and take a moment to really look and feel around yourselves, and one day a tiny miracle *will* happen. Once it does, and you see and accept it for what it is, and open your heart to the vulnerable position of 'trusting', then the floodgates will open and angels will become part of your daily life.

Find Your Angel's Name

So many people write to me asking the name of their angel. It's funny, because angels don't have names as such; as beings of pure energy, they have no need of them. They recognize us and each other by our energy signature, which, like a fingerprint, is unique to each person. However, as humans we sometimes need a focus for our connection, and so angels are quite happy to be given names for our sake.

Here's a nice meditation for discovering your angel's name. I'd like to stress that this name won't actually come from your angel but from your own mind, which already knows the name you want to call your angel. Start your meditation with regular breathing and relaxation. If the breathing isn't enough for you to 'tune out' your chattering mind, here are a few tricks you can use:

- Never drink caffeine or alcohol in the few hours before you do your meditation.
- Don't do your meditation when tired or sleepy, or you will fall asleep.

- Don't try and meditate with the TV or loud music playing.

If you still can't switch off, try thinking of the name of an animal for every letter of the alphabet starting with A. Or, count your breaths backwards in sets of three, starting at 200. Do these things while breathing deeply, and you should find yourself slipping down (or up) into your subconscious. Once this happens, ask for a number. Suppose you come up with the number 25129935. In numerology the following chart shows the letters represented by each of the numbers 1–9:

1	2	3	4	5	6	7	8	9
A	B	C	D	E	F	G	H	I
J	K	L	M	N	O	P	Q	R
S	T	U	V	W	X	Y	Z	

Now this is the fun part! Look at the number you've been given and see what letters flow for you. So the number I suggested, when looked at carefully (bearing in mind you already have the answer in your mind,) could become BEATRICE. Some people might immediately see a name, but for others it could take longer. Once you have a name, look up the meaning of it, because that too will contain a message for you. Beatrice, for instance, means 'blessed traveller'.

Signs and Messages

Angel lights can take many forms. The green ones I described earlier were quite extreme, but your angel sign might be more subtle, such as a bright spot on a wall that has no visible cause or a haze of colour (aura) around some person or object. You might constantly be seeing a specific colour, and if so, look up its meaning for it may be your angel colour.

The most obvious angel sign is a feather, but of course the feather has to be either in a very unusual place, be a very unusual colour or be unusual in the quantity that you find, while not finding a source for them.

You might feel a hand holding yours very gently, or sense a cuddle when you really needed it. You have to be willing to reach out to feel these things, as they will be very subtle. You have to be willing to believe.

If you see your pet's eyes following something unseen around a room, then they may be able to see what you cannot. This can also happen with babies. Be aware that anything that scares your pet or your baby will not be an angel. No one would look upon an angel with any kind of fear.

Some angels manifest a certain scent. This could be flowery, a perfume or even tobacco or chocolate. If you get a strong scent with no apparent cause, this may be your angel. Again, look up the meaning, because that may hold a message for you.

You might be lucky enough to hear your angel sing. This happened to me once in the middle of the night when I was woken by the most beautiful singing I'd ever heard. Of course, your angel might make him- or herself known by some other sound, such as a tinkling bell or a buzzing sound. You might hear the same song on the radio, no matter which station you tune in to. If that's the case, pay particular attention to the lyrics, which will be meaningful to you.

If you find a coin in the street or someone gives you one for no apparent reason, don't ignore it, as it might contain a message from your angel. Look at the date on the coin, and see if it's significant. What metal is it made from? That, too, could have meaning, so look it up. In any case, money, freely given or found, is a sure sign your angel is supporting you.

My husband, Tony, once had a cloud of light sparkles appear above his head and circle around him. This is a great sign that you are going to get exactly what you asked for.

Rainbows are of course a natural phenomenon, but that doesn't mean your angel won't use one to connect with you. If you've asked a question and a rainbow appears, accept that as a positive answer from your angel.

Your angel's presence might cause a sudden drop or rise in temperature. You might suddenly feel like you're standing right in front of a heater. This happened to me when my angel brought through the spirit of my much-loved dog, who had passed over. It even happened live on TV and was felt by the whole crew. Or you could get the shivers, especially at the back of your neck.

The most important sign is probably just that you 'feel' an angel close by, because if you feel one, then one will be there! Confirmation can then come in the form of a whispered message, like the one I received 20 years ago, which dragged me out of depression by guiding me to discover my past life. The most important thing is to accept the messages and signs, because as I said earlier, it will inevitably lead to you discovering more and more of them.

WEEKLY
DIARY
2015

JANUARY

M	T	W	T	F	S	S
			1	2	3	4
5	6	7	8	9	10	11
12	13	14	15	16	17	18
19	20	21	22	23	24	25
26	27	28	29	30	31	

FEBRUARY

M	T	W	T	F	S	S
						1
2	3	4	5	6	7	8
9	10	11	12	13	14	15
16	17	18	19	20	21	22
23	24	25	26	27	28	

MARCH

M	T	W	T	F	S	S
30	31					1
2	3	4	5	6	7	8
9	10	11	12	13	14	15
16	17	18	19	20	21	22
23	24	25	26	27	28	29

APRIL

M	T	W	T	F	S	S
		1	2	3	4	5
6	7	8	9	10	11	12
13	14	15	16	17	18	19
20	21	22	23	24	25	26
27	28	29	30			

MAY

M	T	W	T	F	S	S
			1	2	3	
4	5	6	7	8	9	10
11	12	13	14	15	16	17
18	19	20	21	22	23	24
25	26	27	28	29	30	31

JUNE

M	T	W	T	F	S	S
1	2	3	4	5	6	7
8	9	10	11	12	13	14
15	16	17	18	19	20	21
22	23	24	25	26	27	28
29	30					

JULY

M	T	W	T	F	S	S
		1	2	3	4	5
6	7	8	9	10	11	12
13	14	15	16	17	18	19
20	21	22	23	24	25	26
27	28	29	30	31		

AUGUST

M	T	W	T	F	S	S
31					1	2
3	4	5	6	7	8	9
10	11	12	13	14	15	16
17	18	19	20	21	22	23
24	25	26	27	28	29	30

SEPTEMBER

M	T	W	T	F	S	S
	1	2	3	4	5	6
7	8	9	10	11	12	13
14	15	16	17	18	19	20
21	22	23	24	25	26	27
28	29	30				

OCTOBER

M	T	W	T	F	S	S
			1	2	3	4
5	6	7	8	9	10	11
12	13	14	15	16	17	18
19	20	21	22	23	24	25
26	27	28	29	30	31	

NOVEMBER

M	T	W	T	F	S	S
30						1
2	3	4	5	6	7	8
9	10	11	12	13	14	15
16	17	18	19	20	21	22
23	24	25	26	27	28	29

DECEMBER

M	T	W	T	F	S	S
	1	2	3	4	5	6
7	8	9	10	11	12	13
14	15	16	17	18	19	20
21	22	23	24	25	26	27
28	29	30	31			

January
Focus on Forgiveness

Forgiveness is a very important state of mind when it comes to angel connection, because angels don't thrive in an atmosphere of resentment. Of course you should forgive others for any arguments that took place last year, but forgiving yourself is much more important. It might be hard to imagine that you could be punishing yourself for things you've said and done, but it can happen in many ways – by overeating, by pushing away people who could help you or by not believing you deserve to be happy and therefore subconsciously spoiling what should be happy events. So, concentrate on your good points and set yourself free to enjoy life.

'I forgive myself as my angel forgives me – truly, deeply and completely.'

Jeanette's True Angel Story

When my mum was eight months pregnant with me, she and my dad parted (I was their third child) and mum found herself in the difficult position of having to give birth to me and then have me fostered/adopted. I went to live with a foster mother, and when I was six weeks old my mum took me to a children's home in Suffolk. At 10 months I was fostered by a couple from Essex, and they eventually adopted me when I was three and a half years old.

My home life was not brilliant and I was beaten and abused. Nobody believed me about the abuse, not even my adopted mother, who said it was my fault. At the age of 17 we moved to Watford, and at 19 I met Paul; we got married in July 1982. The only family member to attend my wedding was my oldest adopted brother, who gave me away.

In 1986 I gave birth to Simon, and after that I decided I'd like to trace my birth family. I found my mum and siblings and met them in 1987 (until I started to look I didn't even know I had siblings). In 1992, my brother Trevor traced our dad, to whom I wrote, and in October 1993 I met him and his wife, but we only ever met up twice as I moved shortly after that and we lost touch. In November 1994, Trevor rang to tell me that Dad had cancer of the throat (he was a heavy smoker), and asked if I would visit. I said no (being stubborn and unforgiving) but a month later Trevor asked me again. We lived about 150 miles apart, so again I refused. In January 1995, Trevor rang me to say that Dad was in hospital and asked me to visit him. I said no once more.

One night I had the most amazing dream that we lived above a pub. Mum and Christine (my sister) were inside, Dad was sitting outside having a smoke and Trevor was playing somewhere nearby. Mum called us to come in, and I kept telling Trev to come in, but he wouldn't. It was so real! Then Dad called me over and said, 'You'd better go in', and I replied, 'But Trev won't come in.' Dad said, 'Don't worry about Trevor, I'll get him in. But you'd better go as your mum's calling you.' The love I felt from this man made me know he wouldn't hurt me, and that he LOVED me.

I woke up shortly after and told Paul. Later that morning I was going shopping, and halfway down the road I asked Simon, 'Is my purse in my bag?' He said it wasn't, so we went back home and I found my purse in my bedroom. As I was leaving the house the phone rang. It was Trevor, who told me that Dad had died in the night. I honestly believe that my dad came to me to tell me he loved me.

The angels showed Jeanette that forgiveness of her dad was also the way forward for her. Even though he had died, her dream showed that her dad was still able to visit her and show that he did deserve her forgiveness. Given other circumstances he would undoubtedly have been a great dad, and it was obviously a big regret in his life that he wasn't able to be there for Jeanette.

Pauline's True Animal Angel Story

One day around 12 years ago, I developed stomach-ache. I felt dreadful, and my husband called the doctor who said my stomach was hard and that I should just take two painkillers and go to see him in the morning. At midnight I felt really ill and kept vomiting. In the end an ambulance was called and I was taken to the General Hospital. I was put on a drip as I had gone into shock, and as I was waiting to be transferred to the main hospital for scans, a nurse came in and asked, 'Is that your dog outside – a black dog?' I looked at my husband. I had a black dog but he assured me she was locked in the house.

A few minutes later, a paramedic came in and asked about the dog. I said it wasn't mine. He said, 'But it arrived with you and is sitting outside the door, and it won't move. It's a small black dog.' I repeated that the dog wasn't mine, but people kept asking me about it. I was baffled.

An ambulance came to transfer me, and as they wheeled me out I noticed the small black dog. It came trotting over to me. I don't know why I did this, but I put my arm over the side of the bed and said, 'I am going to be okay – you can go now.' With that the little dog trotted out of the gate and we followed in the ambulance. Through the window I could see that the streets were deserted – it was now the early hours of the morning and we were in a quiet area of town – and the dog had completely disappeared.

When I got to the main hospital I was told I had pancreatitis, which had a 99% mortality rate, and that I might well die. But I told the doctor there was no way I was going to die – after all I had told the little black dog I would be fine. To cut a long story short, I made a recovery that the specialist told me was nothing short of 'a miracle'. I know the angels had come to assist me in the form I would be most familiar with – a dog.

I realized later that the dog had reminded me of one that had been run over outside my home. I'd sat with it, talking to it and stroking its head until the light left its eyes. I think the angels used the dog to thank me for being there, and to remind me that I was special and worth saving.

Angels will manifest in all shapes and forms, and Pauline is quite right that they often choose a persona that they know we'll easily relate to.

Facebook friends and their angels

Angel Ellie says:

'I always use Archangels, and Michael and Raphael in particular. I became more interested in working with Archangels after I saw three of them at the bottom of my bed during a very difficult time in my life.'

DECEMBER/JANUARY *Week 1*

29 Monday

30 Tuesday

31 Wednesday

1 Thursday

Friday   2

Ask your angel to bring you good friends who'll
love, understand and help you through your life.

Saturday   3

Sunday   4

This week's angel colour is **BABY PINK**
– surround yourself with self-love.

Your spirit animal is the **HORSE** –
be a driving force in your own life.

JANUARY *Week 2*

....

5 Monday ○

....

6 Tuesday

....

7 Wednesday

Ask your angel to help you let go of money
worries, so that money can start to flow.

8 Thursday

....

Friday 9

Saturday 10

Sunday 11

This week's angel colour is **PUCE** –
love the natural world today.

Your spirit animal is the **CAT** – look for
magic in your life as it will energize you.

JANUARY *Week 3*

....

12 Monday

....

13 Tuesday ☽

....

14 Wednesday

Ask your angel to let you understand that you
only need your own approval of what you do.
....

15 Thursday

....

Friday 16

Saturday 17

Sunday 18

This week's angel colour is **MAUVE** – feel the depth of your angel's love for you.

Your spirit animal is the **ARMADILLO** – respect others' boundaries, but build your own too.

JANUARY *Week 4*

....

19 Monday

....

20 Tuesday ●

....

21 Wednesday

....

22 Thursday

....

Friday 23

Saturday 24

Ask your angel to help you see the moments
of magic in your everyday life.

Sunday 25

This week's angel colour is **LILAC** – your
angel enfolds you with a gentle hug.

Your spirit animal is the **PRAIRIE DOG** –
recreate bonds with your family.

JANUARY *Week 5*

....

26 Monday

Ask your angel to allow your gratitude for the
past year to spill over you like a warm caress..
....

27 Tuesday ◗

....

28 Wednesday

....

29 Thursday

....

Friday **30**

Saturday **31**

Sunday **1**

This week's angel colour is **DARK GREEN** – you'll
have a sense of growth, harmony and freshness.

Your spirit animal is the **CHEETAH** – things are
moving very fast right now, so don't miss a step.

February
Remember that You Are a Worthy Soul

There are many major prejudices in this world, and they affect a great many people. More insidious are the little prejudices we develop about ourselves. Parental influence, peer pressure, teacher control, management in the workplace, abusive relationships, emotional blackmail – all these things can create feelings of not being worthy and of not fulfilling the expectations of others. If this is holding you back, see yourself through the eyes of your angel. This being knows everything about you, and they see through to your soul and they love you. What could be a greater endorsement of you being a worthy soul than that?

'I deserve all the happiness my angel is willing to give me, and I accept it with gratitude.'

Joan's True Angel Story

Many years ago, I went through a particularly bad time. My husband, who had been having an affair for many years, was leaving me, and I would be homeless, jobless and penniless, with three children to bring up. He also told lies about the situation. He went on holiday, taking two of our children, and I decided to spend the only money I had taking my daughter on a holiday so that she didn't miss out. The holiday was difficult, but we do have some good memories of that time.

The day we were due to travel home I cried and cried. I don't remember the journey. I just remember arriving at the train station. We climbed off the train into a crowd of people. My emotions were everywhere – I didn't want to return and I was worried about my children. You can imagine the situation. The crowd was heading in the same direction, but suddenly, blocking my way, was a very well-dressed gentleman with piercing blue eyes and tanned skin. He stood looking into my eyes. He was dressed for our English weather but he looked really bronzed, and the power of his eyes made me stop and listen to him.

He simply said, 'You will be alright.'

He walked past me, and all I can say is that he just 'disappeared'.

My immediate reaction was to reply, 'What do you know?' but something told me not to say it, and there was no time to reply anyway. I thought, how does he know what's happening? Did I talk about my situation on the train and he overheard? But I know I didn't, because I didn't want to upset my daughter.

I looked for the man, hoping to ask what had made him say that to me, but he had gone.

The years have passed and I have been alright – life led me towards being a therapist and tutor and I love working with energies. Every day I ask the angels to help me, and now know that this gentleman was Archangel Michael. I feel very humble that he should appear to me. And I know that the angels love us and want to help us if we ask for it.

Joan was obviously feeling unworthy and desperate, unloved and abandoned, which happens to so many of us at some point during our lives. If things had gone unchanged, her future, and that of her children, could have been very bleak, so the angel came at exactly the right time. Joan shouldn't really feel humble that an angel should select her to visit, because all the angels love us unconditionally, and see our true, worthy selves.

Athena's True Animal Angel Story

For many years we owned two cats, Jelly and Delilah. They were very special, and Jelly in particular appeared to be telepathic. One night, when he was about 10 years old, he sat in the lounge and cried and cried for no apparent reason. He cried so much for about 30 minutes, rooted to the spot, that we got quite worried about him. Then he stopped as quickly as he'd started.

The next day I telephoned his breeder to tell her what had happened. She lives 10 miles away. She told me that at the exact time that Jelly started to cry, his father, Parker, had passed away. It was quite sudden, and there was no reason for it. She was badly shocked and very upset at the time of my call. Could Jelly have sensed it? We don't know, but whatever the reason for his cries that night, they were so sad to hear.

Then, two weeks before Jelly passed away, his mother, Adeline, passed away aged 19. She and Jelly were close, as we always took Jelly back to the same breeder for boarding, and Jelly and Adeline would meet and kiss noses. We felt that Jelly could sense that his mother had passed, because after that he seemed to lose the will to carry on. We feel sure that our beloved Jelly was telepathic. Both of our beautiful cats, Jelly and Delilah, passed over within a couple of months of each other, aged 18. We were both distraught, but your book, Pets Have Souls Too, *has given us hope that our beloved Jelly and*

Delilah are both well and at peace over the Rainbow Bridge. Initially we both felt that to get another cat would betray the memory of Jelly and Delilah, but your book has taught us so much and we have now decided to get two kittens in the new year. God willing we will have two beautiful kittens to love again, and they will bring back to our house the warmth it currently lacks without our beloved Jelly and Delilah.

I liked this story, in particular because it demonstrates that animals are just as worthy as we humans are, and in some ways more so. How different the world would be if we looked at our animals the way our angels do. Animals are striving to help the world right now, and they will help us change if we see the angels in them.

Facebook friends and their angels

Lynn Kilparick says:

'I talk to all the Archangels and my own personal angel too. When I feel down or need support, I ask for help and then feel a warm breeze envelop me. I get answers too through songs and numbers.'

Friday 30

Saturday 31

Sunday 1

This week's angel colour is **DARK GREEN** – you'll have a sense of growth, harmony and freshness.

Your spirit animal is the **CHEETAH** – things are moving very fast right now, so don't miss a step.

FEBRUARY *Week 6*

2 Monday

Pagan festival of Imbolc: a celebration of the sun's gradual
return. It's a time of rebirth, of our sun and of us.

3 Tuesday ○

4 Wednesday

Ask your angel to help you find
balance in all areas of your life.

5 Thursday

Friday 6

Saturday 7

Sunday 8

This week's angel colour is **ROYAL BLUE**
– have honour when others lose theirs.

Your spirit animal is the **GOAT** – always
stay grounded, with a firm foundation.

FEBRUARY *Week 7*

....

9 Monday

....

10 Tuesday

....

11 Wednesday

♥ Ask your angel to show you how to
manifest your own reality.

....

12 Thursday ◑

....

Week 7 FEBRUARY

Friday 13

Saturday 14

Sunday 15

This week's angel colour is **BLACK**
– shut the door on dark past events for good.

Your spirit animal is the **PANTHER** – understand
that sometimes you need to welcome change.

FEBRUARY *Week 8*

....

16 Monday

....

17 Tuesday

....

18 Wednesday ●

....

19 Thursday

....

Friday 20

Saturday 21

Ask your angel to help you be
adventurous and not fear change.

Sunday 22

This week's angel colour is **SALMON PINK** – return
to old haunts in your mind and rediscover yourself.

Your spirit animal is the **VOLE** – listen very
carefully to what your soul tells you.

FEBRUARY *Week 9*

....

23 Monday

♥ Ask your angel to watch over you while
you move forwards with your life.

....

24 Tuesday

....

25 Wednesday ◑

....

26 Thursday

....

Friday 27

Saturday 28

Sunday 1

This week's angel colour is **ORANGE** – the
sun always shines around your angel.

Your spirit animal is the **OCELOT** –
don't keep others at a distance.

March
Live in the Now

This is one area in which the angels in our pets can show us a better way. Animals don't focus on problems, don't worry about the future and they don't worry about how long they'll live. Some people would say that's just because they're not self-aware. Well, of course they are self-aware, as scientists are realizing more and more. Animals live in the NOW, because it comes naturally to them. In contrast, we humans find this very difficult. We either dwell in the past, which no longer exists, or we live in the future, which does not yet exist. The happiest people in the world are those who exist totally in the moment, for they are the only ones living in reality.

'I live in the NOW, because if I do not then I miss out on life, and it will pass me by.'

Jenny's True Angel Story

Several years ago I'd been sinking into depression, and I couldn't see any way to stop the downward spiral. There was no real reason for it, just little things, but I'm told that's often the way with depression. It slowly builds until it becomes the norm to feel that way. One night I was in bed, unable to sleep or to see any light at the end of the tunnel. I was thinking about the next day, about how hard it was going to be to find the enthusiasm just to get up. My energy was low, dull and static, and maybe that stillness is why my angel was able to come to me.

The first thing I noticed was a column of light in the corner of the room. It was deep purple, not really shiny or bright, but just there, slowly rotating. I was a bit shocked at first and waited for it to disappear, but it didn't. After a few seconds the light started to glow and spread towards me. As it enveloped me I experienced a feeling of great calm, followed by euphoria, and it was at that point I realized there was an angel in the room. I then felt the total love emanating from this being – love for me – and I shivered in delight. I felt humbled and exalted at the same time. Then a deep, strong voice asked, 'Are you happy?' 'Yes!' I answered immediately, out loud.

'Are you sure?' the voice asked. 'Is there nothing troubling you?'

'No', I answered truthfully, and the realization hit me that it was true. With this being here, sending me love all the time, my problems seemed insignificant, laughable even. What else could matter after this?

'Will you be happy tomorrow?' the voice asked.

That was a little more difficult. 'Err… if you are here I will be.' My heart sank a little at this point as I realized I might never be happy again without this being by my side.

'The choice is yours,' the angel said. 'You can choose to be happy or not. Your state of mind is up to you. I am always here, I have always been here, I will always be here. You just have to be alive in every moment and you will know this.'

And it was true, I finally understood that the angels are always there for us, always loving us, and the choice of 'knowing' that is up to us, every second of every day. Once you know this, then you can choose to be happy, no matter what.

Jenny gives us a great example of how angels will bring us what we need instead of what we think we want.

George's True Animal Angel Story

I've never been a big fan of animals to be honest; I was even afraid of sheep! But something happened to change all that. I'd always rushed about, tearing through life at breakneck speed, and that's really what I thought it was all about. I was probably brought up to think that – called lazy and told to 'hurry up' the whole time. I never had time for pets, not even for romance or children. I just rushed about all the time.

Then one day I was driving and a little dog ran out in front of my van. I wasn't mad about animals but I didn't want to kill one, so I braked hard, hopped out of the van and picked her up. I knocked on doors, trying to find the pup's owner. I even called vets and the police, but no one could tell me where she'd come from. She was a mixed breed, mostly grey and fluffy, but also cold and wet. There had been a big storm the night before, and I can only think she literally got blown there! What else could I call her but Windy?

Windy took over my life. I had to make time to walk her, feed her and play with her. I laughed at her and with her. I had to clear up after her, buy her food, take her to the vets – the whole thing. One friend asked me why I kept her, why I didn't take her to the RSPCA or something. I had no answer. It just was what it was.

After observing how happy Windy was with so little – a kind word, a biscuit, a cuddle – I found myself thinking, this is the way I should be: happy with the moment I'm in. *It clicked. I changed, and since Windy came along, I'm happier than ever before. And romance? There's nothing like a cute puppy to get girls talking to you! I honestly think someone 'up there' who cares sent her to me, to change me, and now I enjoy life instead of just racing through it.*

George's story illustrates several things perfectly: how angels will find ways to help us that we never would have imagined for ourselves; how an animal can be angel-sent; and how, if we just let them into our lives, animals really can help us to change our lives for the better.

Facebook friends and their angels

Keeley Louise Fitzsimmons says:

'I tend to connect with angels via dreams. I'll ask my question before I go to bed and the answers come in the night. At the moment I'm pregnant, and I'm calling on Sandalphon, the Archangel who delivers our prayers to heaven.'

Friday 27

Saturday 28

Sunday 1

This week's angel colour is **ORANGE** – the
sun always shines around your angel.

Your spirit animal is the **OCELOT** –
don't keep others at a distance.

MARCH *Week 10*

....

2 Monday

....

3 Tuesday

♥ Ask your angel to help you break down old
destructive patterns and see new opportunities.
....

4 Wednesday

....

5 Thursday ○

....

Friday 6

Saturday 7

Sunday 8

This week's angel colour is **DAFFODIL YELLOW** –
feel the sun on your face and be thankful you can.

Your spirit animal is the **COW** – find joy
and fulfilment in family and home.

MARCH *Week 11*

....

9 Monday

....

10 Tuesday

....

11 Wednesday

Ask your angel to allow you to let go of anything
you need to give up and seek transformation.
....

12 Thursday

....

◑ Friday 13

Saturday 14

Sunday 15

This week's angel colour is **GREY** – your angel will bring a glimmer of hope.

Your spirit animal is the **LION** – strengthen your intention to resolve your problems.

MARCH *Week 12*

16 Monday

17 Tuesday

Ask your angel to bring you harmonious
relationships and fruitful commitments.

18 Wednesday

19 Thursday

● Friday 20

Pagan Festival of Ostara – Spring Equinox. Thanksgiving for the return of life and the start of a brand new cycle.

Saturday 21

Sunday 22

This week's angel colour is **MINT GREEN** – let your angel refresh your soul.

Your spirit animal is the **RAT** – be adaptable and resourceful in a changing environment.

MARCH *Week 13*

....

23 Monday

....

24 Tuesday

....

25 Wednesday

....

26 Thursday

....

● Friday 27

Saturday 28

Ask your angel to help you build on the foundations you've worked so hard for.

Sunday 29

This week's angel colour is **AQUA** – travel beckons you to new horizons. Be brave!

Your spirit animal is the **DOG** – don't be afraid to support and protect those you love.

30 Monday

31 Tuesday

1 Wednesday

Ask your angel to give you abundant energy
so that you can work and play equally hard.

2 Thursday

April
Spring into a Life of Fun

Some people take angels too seriously. It took
me about three years before I realized that they
actually have a pretty good sense of humour, and
when you think of the messes we humans get into
sometimes, you can see why they'd need to. So,
at this time of year when new life is springing up
all around, we should try and do the same. Not
necessarily by creating new life ourselves, although
that would work, but by putting more life into what
we do. Remember, faith = no stress, and stress =
no faith. Relax and enjoy what's going on around
you, and if that's not enjoyable right now, have
faith that it will get better with the help of your
angels, and then you can at least be stress free.

'When all else fails me my angels
will not, and I can feel their warm
caress whenever I choose.'

Pauline's True Angel Story

I'd always suffered migraine headaches as a teenager, and I was literally useless for about three days. I had medication, but nothing helped. I remember a time in my early 20s when I left work with a really bad headache. I couldn't wait to get home, but had to drive carefully as my vision was blurred. I reached a junction where the traffic lights were red. I waited, and when they turned green I was about to drive off when a voice behind me said, very loudly, 'Look to your left – he's not going to stop.' So I looked, and a large car overshot the red light. I was in a small Triumph Spitfire, and if I had moved off the larger car would have hit me. I would have stood no chance at all.

I never thought to ignore the voice, but I had no idea where it came from. I got home and told Mum that my head hurt so much that I could barely hold it up. I nodded off, but the pain kept waking me. I had no painkillers and was beginning to feel very sick. Just then a person appeared in front of me, holding a glass of water and something in their other hand. I presumed, in my pain, that it was Mum, as my vision was blurred and the room was dark. I took the glass and she put two tablets into my hand. 'Take these,' she said. I took them, drank half the glass of water and put the glass on the floor next to my bed. She then helped me lie down and started stroking my head saying, 'There, there, you'll be alright in the morning.' I went to sleep with her still stroking my forehead.

Next morning I woke refreshed with no headache and no nausea; in fact, I got up and ate a cooked breakfast. My mum came down and asked how I was feeling. I said, 'Those tablets you brought me were amazing – what were they?' Mum looked puzzled and said, 'But I don't have any painkillers, and I didn't come to your room during the night.' I pointed to the half-full glass of water, but Mum was adamant and I realized it couldn't have been her. She has short grey curls, and the person who visited me during the night had long, wavy hair right down her back. She was also younger. I presume this was my guardian angel. There's no other explanation for it.'

When people have faith in the presence of their angels, it makes them open and receptive to help like this.

Natascha's True Animal Angel Story

In 2009, my cats Marie and Ninjo became parents to three kittens. Before giving birth, Marie waited for my husband to come home with our dog, Rocky, and Ninjo was sitting with her. My husband and I held her paws throughout. It was beautiful to be with our cat while she gave birth, and that Ninjo stayed with her too. Then our little girls Molly, Minou and Lillifee came to earth.

Molly and Minou spent a lot of time together, but Minou was with me very often. When it was bedtime, Minou led us across the hall, meow-ing as if to say, 'Come on, it's sleepy time!'

Molly was more independent and strong willed, but she was always close to us as well. Each night she'd lie down on my chest for exactly 20 minutes.

Later we moved into my parents' house. A strange cat suffering from a cold was in our garden and we all got sick. Marie, Ninjo and Lillifee recovered pretty quickly, and Minou seemed normal as well, eating and behaving as she usually did. Only Molly was very ill. She barely ate, spent a lot of time crouched down on the floor and she stopped cleaning herself. Of course we went to the vet several times, but all he could do was prescribe antibiotics. Molly could not take anything in her mouth, since it had become a huge mycosis. She got worse and worse.

One afternoon I heard my husband yelling from the living room. I ran in, fearing the worst from his scream. Minou was in the armchair she'd been born in, dead. It was as if the pain would rip us apart. I had not seen this coming – Minou had seemed well, in contrast to her sister Molly, who looked sick all that time. The fear of losing Molly as well kept us from sleep. She was always with us in the bedroom and slept on one of us, in case we would need to react quickly.

We searched for other vets, but none could help. And then the day came when, looking back, we now know that Molly said farewell to us. Suddenly she ran around, ate something and lay down in the sun. Her father, Marie and Lillifee were all with her, and I also lay down next to her. I saw that she was looking me in the eye, and I sensed there was something in her sight – as though she had already taken a look at the other side. Before I realized what was happening, she looked at my husband and then at me, and we suddenly knew she was about to leave us.

We'll always be grateful for the time we spent with Molly and Minou, and that Molly let us take part in her departure. We buried them both in our back yard as their father, Ninjo, watched from afar. He grieved for a long time afterwards.

Nowadays Molly and Minou are with us again. Their sister, Lillifee, has had two babies – Sweeney, in whom Molly lives on, and a tomcat, Finley, who embodies Minou. An important sign for us is Ninjo's relationship with Finley. He usually hates other tomcats, but they both snuggle like he and Minou did back in the day. And Finley is always by my side, like Minou was back then. My husband and I have always *been certain that the two would return and they have, each with their own character.*

Natascha never lost faith that her pets would return, and so she was not only able to cope with the terrible loss in as stress-free a way as possible, but she was ready to have faith enough to recognize them when they did return.

Facebook friends and their angels

Jade Mitchell says:

'When I'm in danger and unaware, or sense I shouldn't go somewhere, I feel a presence. For example, when I go to cross the road and can't see, sometimes it's like someone's in front of me, holding me back.'

30 Monday

31 Tuesday

1 Wednesday

Ask your angel to give you abundant energy
so that you can work and play equally hard.

2 Thursday

Friday   3

○ Saturday   4

Sunday   5

This week's angel colour is **GOLD** – you are a winner in every sense with your angel beside you!

Your spirit animal is the **DONKEY** – go with the flow and allow your angels to do their work.

APRIL *Week 15*

. . . .

6 Monday

. . . .

7 Tuesday

Ask your angel to bring you joy
and emotional security.

8 Wednesday

. . . .

9 Thursday

. . . .

Friday 10

Saturday 11

◑ Sunday 12

This week's angel colour is **LEMON** – don't fear
that sharp word, you can absorb it without harm.

Your spirit animal is the **BADGER** – be
persistent in your goals but ready to adapt.

APRIL *Week 16*

....

13 Monday

....

14 Tuesday

....

15 Wednesday

....

16 Thursday

....

Friday 17

Ask your angel to help you organize your
time better so that stress is lifted.

● Saturday 18

Sunday 19

This week's angel colour is **DARK BROWN** –
feel regal, as you are always royal to your angel.

Your spirit animal is the **SHEEP** – make sure
you remain sensitive to the feelings of others.

APRIL *Week 17*

. . . .

20 Monday

. . . .

21 Tuesday

Ask your angel to help you maintain a positive
mindset and choose to be happy, no matter what.

. . . .

22 Wednesday

. . . .

23 Thursday

. . . .

Friday 24

Saturday 25

● Sunday 26

This week's angel colour is **BRIGHT GREEN** – smell the grass and feel privileged to live on this planet.

Your spirit animal is the **BEAR** – don't be afraid to be a leader rather than a follower.

APRIL *Week 18*

....

27 Monday

....

28 Tuesday

♥ Ask your angel to increase your intuitive powers so that you understand others more easily.

....

29 Wednesday

....

30 Thursday

....

May
Sow Seeds for Success

Now you can start creating the life you want to live, but given that this is the year in which everyone should strive towards balance, it can be difficult to sort out what you need from what you want. So, be specific, and if what you asked for doesn't come along, try and have faith to accept that it wasn't what you needed. As humans we often don't really know what we need to make us feel happy and fulfilled, and so faith in your angels is essential. If a door appears to close that you were expecting to walk through, look for the open window, because your angels will never leave you helpless.

'With the help of my angels I'll
become balanced and focused
in every area of my life.'

Amelya's True Angel Story

I've always read about the 'lucky ones' who get a sign from their angels. For so long I've hoped for a sign that my angels are with me, and finally I got one! I've been trying to get myself balanced, both physically and spiritually, and so I've been having crystal healing and reflexology.

My most recent treatment was very dramatic, and afterwards the lady who treated me was very excited. She couldn't wait to show me what she'd seen while she was doing the treatment. She'd put a glass of water on the floor before she started the healing, and during the treatment she'd noticed something underneath it that wasn't there before. She picked up the glass and showed me the big, white feather that was there. There was no way it could have got there by itself, because the doors and windows were all closed. It was a massive sign from the angels!

I told her how I'd kept reading about other people having a white feather mysteriously appear from nowhere as a sign from the angels, but it had never happened to me before! Wow, the energy was so strong after that happened!

Right now our angels really want us to try to be balanced, and it goes to show that if you do what your angels would like, then they will send you a sign in confirmation that you have their approval.

Margaret's True Animal Angel Story

When my husband, Toby, died unexpectedly aged 42, I was of course devastated, but Toby had rescued me from an abusive relationship, and the five short years I'd had with him weren't really enough to make me feel secure. My ex had tried to track me down on several occasions and I was very afraid at night, petrified that someone would break in, so I rarely slept. I used to pile saucepans in front of all the doors, thinking it would give me an early warning if someone tried to break in. It all got too much. A friend suggested I get a dog, but my ex had a big dog he used to terrorize me with, so I was afraid of them too.

In the end, because Toby had left me the smallholding where we lived, although it might sound mad, I got an alpaca. I'd been told they were very territorial and a lot of farmers put them in with their sheep to chase foxes away, and apparently they were very good at it. The problem was that alpacas don't make a lot of noise, so I still wouldn't know if anything happened during the night. The alpaca did make me feel a lot better though.

A couple of months later I was looking at our photo albums.

I'd been looking at one photo of Toby in particular – he was younger, and standing with a flock of geese. He'd told me that he loved those geese, and they were always gentle with him, even though they used to chase and peck other people. He'd also said they were great lawn mowers, and I certainly needed one of them. Anyway, I went to sleep and dreamed that Toby was there with me. Nothing unusual about that; I did it all the time. But what was odd was that in his arms he was carrying a gosling, all fluffy and cute, and he held it out to me. I woke up thinking I was holding it, and I felt quite bereft when I realized it wasn't really there. This helped me decide what to do next.

I did some research and discovered that geese are said to be excellent watchdogs. So I bought twenty goslings, including a gander, and as they grew they all became attached to me. They were always gentle and never pecked me. But, sure enough, I had to shut them away when I had visitors or the geese would attack them. After a few times of watching my friends dive into the house with the gander close on their heels, shouting at the top of his voice, I gave the geese the run of the land and barns at night, and I never really worried again.

I'm totally (well, almost) convinced that Toby, the one person who helped me regain my sense of perspective and confidence had returned once more, to show me how to achieve peace of mind.

Despite the obvious tragedies in her life, Margaret was well on her way to becoming balanced and well rounded. I'm sure that Toby will be watching over her for the rest of her life, even though I have an idea that there's another mate out there for her somewhere. Perhaps the geese (or Toby) will lead her to him, and it will happen as soon as she stops being afraid.

Facebook friends and their angels

Sue Fensome says:

'I sense my hair being touched when I'm feeling down, and if I ask a question I always find a penny or see butterflies.'

Friday 1

Pagan Festival of Beltane: the day that commemorates
the Union between God and Goddess.

Saturday 2

Sunday 3

This week's angel colour is **BABY BLUE**
– remember how it felt to be a child.

Your spirit animal is the **PUMA** – be strong
and unyielding so that your power will grow.

MAY *Week 19*

....

4 Monday ○

♥ Ask your angel to bring you clarity of
mind so that decisions are easy.
....

5 Tuesday

....

6 Wednesday

....

7 Thursday

....

Friday 8

Saturday 9

Sunday 10

This week's angel colour is **SCARLET** – feel passionate about spreading the word about angels.

Your spirit animal is the **BAT** – your angel will help you navigate the unknown.

MAY *Week 20*

....

11 Monday ☽

....

12 Tuesday

....

13 Wednesday

♥ Ask your angel to bring you a more laid back
and less chaotic life, to slow down time.
....

14 Thursday

....

Friday 15

Saturday 16

Sunday 17

This week's angel colour is **SILVER** – treat
your body to a cleansing with colloidal silver.

Your spirit animal is the **GIRAFFE** – take care of
what you say and how it might affect others.

MAY *Week 21*

....

18 Monday ●

....

19 Tuesday

....

20 Wednesday

....

21 Thursday

....

Friday 22

Saturday 23

Ask your angel to increase your creativity
so that new ideas spring to mind.

Sunday 24

This week's angel colour is **BURNT ORANGE**
– fan the flames and discover an exciting future.

Your spirit animal is the **PENGUIN** – your angel
will guide you in dreams through the astral plane.

MAY *Week 22*

....

25 Monday ◑

....

26 Tuesday

♥ Ask your angel to help you re-evaluate
your life on a regular basis.
....

27 Wednesday

....

28 Thursday

....

Friday 29

Saturday 30

Sunday 31

This week's angel colour is **DEEP RED** – take
action rather than delaying the inevitable.

Your spirit animal is the **EAGLE** – try looking
at life from a different perspective.

~∽⌒o⌒∽~

June
Get into the Holiday Spirit

~∽⌒℮⌒∽~

*This month I want you to give yourself a holiday.
I know an actual holiday isn't always possible,
with financial implications and time off work,
but a virtual holiday is always possible with the
help of your angels. Ask them to help you give
yourself permission to have a virtual break from
your problems and worries; take at least a week
off from them. Give yourself permission to stop
feeling guilty about anything, stop being worried
about anything, stop having panic attacks and
stop worrying about health. In fact, stop worrying
about anything. If you can do this consistently
for a whole week, you'll be surprised what a
difference it might make in your whole life.*

*'I give myself permission to allow
the whole of my being to come first
in my life, if only for a while.'*

Pauline's Son's True Angel Story

I was driving to work along a busy road when, all of a sudden, a car pulled out from a small side road right in front of me. I braked, but it was no use, and I knew I was going to hit the other car. I thought my time was up. In the rear-view mirror I saw a young boy with blonde curls sitting on the back seat, but thought nothing further and just shut my eyes, waiting for the impact.

The next few seconds were a blur. When I opened my eyes, my car had turned 180 degrees and was facing the other way. The steering wheel had hit me in the chest, and the engine had been pushed through the passenger side. I suddenly thought, Oh no, my passenger in the back seat! *But then I remembered I'd been on my way to work – alone. There was no sign of a child anywhere, in or outside the car.*

I got out of my car, and drivers coming the other way were congratulating me on my driving skills, saying that my car had spun around and around and yet somehow I'd avoided each and every one of them. I knew that my eyes had been closed the whole time. Then the police arrived and asked, 'Where's the driver?' I said, 'It was me! I'm the driver,' and a police officer told me I should be dead.

I was taken to hospital and diagnosed with whiplash and a bruised sternum where the steering wheel had hit my chest, but that was all. My mum told me the child in the back seat was my guardian angel, and that he had steered the car for me so I'd have no further impacts. I'm not sure if I believe it, but Mum does.

This story suits the light-hearted month of June. No one was really hurt, and it's kind of funny that Pauline's son can accept that a strange child appeared and then vanished from the back seat, but not believe in angels. It's often the way, but whether we believe in angels or not, if they're meant to, then they will help us.

Trudy-Ann's True Animal Angel Story

Nothing is as scary as accidentally wandering into the wrong part of town, and suddenly realizing that a gang of strange-looking men with hoodies, tattoos and piercings are following you in the shadows. Then the realization hits you that you don't know where you are or how to escape, and you feel like you're about to die, or worse. This was what happened to me once in Nashville. When you think of Nashville, you think of country music, cowboys, (well, singing cowboys) and good fun had by all in a family atmosphere. That had been my impression anyway, but I found out that evening that Nashville has its dark secrets, just like any other city.

I'd gone for a walk and detoured away from where I needed to be, just to have a look around. The street wasn't well lit and I should have turned around as soon as I realized I was lost. But I kept thinking, it's not such a huge place, and if I keep heading in the same direction I'll eventually find my way to somewhere I recognize. So, there I was – lost, alone, vulnerable, very scared and being tailed by about 10 young men, who I'm sure didn't want to help me find my way.

I couldn't hear their actual words, but I got the gist of what they were saying and could tell they were egging each other on. I kept walking, moving fast but trying to look like I wasn't panicking. They moved faster to match me, and I ended up trotting along so it was obvious that I was panicking. It got worse when I heard their footsteps break into a run, and like a deer with a pack of wolves on her tail I knew I was about to be brought down.

It's interesting that wolves should have crossed my mind at that point, because two things then happened at once. I'd been on my way to a talk on guardian angels when I got lost, and right then I saw one in my mind's eye, together with the wolves, and I randomly begged them all for help. The footsteps got closer, and as I passed under a streetlight I thought I would *feel a hand close around my shoulder, but instead there was a sudden and abrupt silence. I ran another 100 metres and then stopped, panting, and looked back. By now I was exhausted and couldn't run any further.*

Back there, under the streetlight I'd passed, stood the gang, staring after me. At first I couldn't understand why they'd stopped, and then I saw movement in the shadows between us. A pair of small green lights hovered there. I don't know why, but I immediately knew they were the eyes of a wolf. How a wolf had got onto the back streets of Nashville I do not know.

The green lights followed me as I started to walk on, keeping an exact distance between the gang and me. I didn't feel any threat from the wolf at all. The wolf never appeared clearly under the streetlights as I passed them, but I knew it was there, and so did the gang. Eventually I turned a corner and, miraculously, I was on a brightly lit street, with people, and I was safe! I looked back into the darker street and I couldn't see the wolf or the gang. I am certain my angel sent a wolf to save me, or appeared as a wolf. Either way I was saved.

Even though Trudy-Ann's situation was very frightening, I think her angel had a great sense of humour to send the very animal she was comparing to her hunters at that moment. And I like to imagine the amusing look on the men's faces as they saw a menacing wolf between them and their prey.

Facebook friends and their angels

Sers Ses says:

'My angels come to me through loved ones, like my mother and my dog, Toffee. Sometimes they come through someone I never knew at all, but I manage to open my heart to that energy. Some people call it 'coincidence', but it's always too detailed to be so.'

JUNE *Week 23*

....

1 Monday

♥ Ask your angel to help others see how
bright and intelligent you really are.

....

2 Tuesday ○

....

3 Wednesday

....

4 Thursday

....

Friday 5

Saturday 6

Sunday 7

This week's angel colour is **TAN** – angels can
help with anything, even holidays in the sun!

Your spirit animal is the **HYENA** –
cultivate the 'team player' in you.

JUNE *Week 24*

....

8 Monday

....

9 Tuesday ☽

Ask your angels to reignite your drive and
ambition to make your dreams come true.
....

10 Wednesday

....

11 Thursday

....

Friday 12

Saturday 13

Sunday 14

This week's angel colour is **WHITE** – be an
angel to someone by giving words of kindness.

Your spirit animal is the **ELEPHANT** – be strong
but gentle and fortune will smile on you.

JUNE *Week 25*

15 Monday

Ask your angels to help you release your
stubbornness and accept help that's being offered.

16 Tuesday ●

17 Wednesday

18 Thursday

....

Friday 19

....

Saturday 20

....

Sunday 21

Pagan Festival of Litha – Summer Solstice. The longest day
of the year, and when the very first crops are gathered.
....

This week's angel colour is **PURPLE** –
listen deeply to your intuitive side.

Your spirit animal is the **PIG** – respect
the mysteries of nature.

JUNE *Week 26*

....

22 Monday

....

23 Tuesday

....

24 Wednesday ◑

....

25 Thursday

....

Friday 26

Saturday 27

Ask your angel to create a home for you
where you'll feel safe and loved at all times.

Sunday 28

This week's angel colour is **LIME
GREEN** – rekindle your zest for life.

Your spirit animal is the **HARE** – be aware that
not everyone is honest. Trust your angel.

....

29 Monday

....

30 Tuesday

....

1 Wednesday

Ask your angel to help you find inner calm
and serenity so that life flows naturally.
....

2 Thursday ○

....

July
Take a Leap of Faith

You've made a fresh start, worked hard on yourself and now given yourself a break. This is the time to start making things happen. If you have a dream, build on it; if you're miserable, this is the time to change things; if you're in a rut, start digging yourself out. People speak about creating your own reality and taking responsibility for things not being what you hoped. It's not easy to create your own life, but it can be done. *So, tell your angel you're ready to take a leap of faith with them. This means making a concerted effort to connect with your angel, and then listening to them, believing them and taking* action *in certain faith that you can make things change – and they will!*

'I just need faith in the guidance I'm given and then I'll have the power to change my life.'

Angela's True Angel Story

We all go through periods of our lives when everything seems to be conspiring against us. Take me for instance; I desperately wanted to move to the countryside. All my readings and angel messages had confirmed that's what I was supposed to do, so why was it so hard? It took me 18 months to sell my house, and until then there'd been loads of houses I wanted to buy, so I thought, at last, it's happening! But the houses I'd liked had all been sold, and there were very few on the market that I liked.

Then, when spring came and more houses appeared, it got really weird. Every time (and I mean at least a dozen times) I found one I liked, one of three things immediately happened. Either another buyer appeared and outbid me; or the owners mysteriously decided not to sell; or they decided to put the property up for auction, or to go to private tender. I bid on several, but I was always the second highest bidder and so I lost out. I got very angry at the spirit world and my angels, asking, 'If I'm meant to do it, why aren't you helping me?'

This went on for months until I was sure I'd lose my buyer, but I didn't, so I thought I must be on the right track and should just have faith. Then suddenly I understood. It turned out that unbeknownst to me, my daughter was not only expecting my first grandchild, but she was also thinking about moving to France to give her child a better life. When I did find out, and she and her husband asked me if I wanted to go too, I immediately found a perfect house near to their new one, and for a much lower price than I would have paid in the UK. I could afford a much bigger house with land, so, it seemed my angels did know what they were doing and were stopping me from making an expensive mistake!

Oh, this sort of thing has happened to me so many times in my life, I can totally see where Angela's coming from. I try really hard now to state my wishes and then go with the flow, because what might seem like a torturously long journey to reach your goals often works out to have been for the best in the end.

Joyce's True Angel Story

The night I finally plucked up courage to leave my abusive husband, I found myself in the street with the front door locked in my face. I'd been given no time to pack anything and had only the clothes I stood up in, and no money. There was a shelter in town, but that was five miles away and it was snowing. I'd just about given up when a cab crawled past. The tail lights winked on and I ran towards it. Initially I stopped myself from getting in though, because I had no money to pay the fare.

Much to my surprise the driver was a woman. Not only did she take me for free, but the journey, which should have taken 20 minutes, actually took two hours. It was as though time stood still, and this gave me a chance to unburden myself. The woman told me I was not to blame, and she left me with a feeling that I had a good future; she somehow also raised my self-esteem sky high with her words, and I walked into the shelter feeling like a new woman. I turned back at the door to wave at the departing cab, but the street was empty.

Angels can appear in many forms, but this is the first cab driver I've come across.

Patty's True Animal Angel Story

It's possible to change your life by changing the lives of others. In my case everything changed because I got involved in rescuing dogs – in other words, changing the dogs' lives. It started when I adopted a dog, really out of sheer desperation for company and something to do. I did it because my family had all passed away and I found it very difficult to make friends in the city where I lived. I felt quite depressed, pretty resentful and fairly angry that I felt so unloved and unimportant in the world.

I soon learned a valuable life lesson. Sasha, my first dog, taught me that you might be able to hide your true feelings from everyone, even yourself, but you cannot hide them from your dog. Your dog observes you all the time. Your dog will react to your inner feelings, and not be fooled by the act you show the world. Your dog will never hold a grudge because you shouted at him, and he will never judge you.

I started to modify my behaviour, as I realized I had been pushing people away for fear of being hurt or judged. Now they would often stop and talk to me because they liked the look of my dog. I had Sasha until he died aged 16 years, which is pretty good for a dog, but it wasn't long enough for me. When he died I nearly went back to square one and retreated into my hermit's shell, but even after he died, Sasha still observed me. I could feel him and smell him, and sometimes I could even hear him snuffling.

So I did the only thing I knew would work, and I adopted another elderly dog. I chose older dogs because I always found it hard to resist their soft eyes, their acceptance of their lot and the deep sadness I felt that they had ended up alone at the time of their life when they really needed love and understanding. Also, of course, most people chose the pups or young dogs, and there were so many wonderful older dogs that deserved to be chosen. Nowadays I also work hard at the shelter, trying to repay all the dogs I meet for being my angels.

At the start of this diary I mentioned that it would be nice if more people adopted older dogs, and Patty's story illustrates just how rewarding this can be.

Facebook friends and their angels

Jan Lewandowski says:

'I've been lucky enough to see one of my angels, who came during one of the most stressful and frightening times of my life. I'd just gone to bed when, in the light from a streetlight, I saw my angel appear beside the bed. He was incredibly tall, reaching almost to the ceiling, and I was filled with total calmness. I've had a rough ride over the past few years, but knowing you have an angel by your side helps you to get through the tough times.'

JUNE/JULY *Week 27*

....

29 Monday

....

30 Tuesday

....

1 Wednesday

Ask your angel to help you find inner calm
and serenity so that life flows naturally.
....

2 Thursday ○

Friday 3

Saturday 4

Sunday 5

This week's angel colour is **PEACH** – the colour of
humility, so don't believe you know everything.

Your spirit animal is the **DEER** – this week no
obstacles will hinder your graceful movement.

JULY *Week 28*

. . . .

6 Monday

Ask your angels to make you a more warm, open and
friendly person interested in the welfare of others.
. . . .

7 Tuesday

. . . .

8 Wednesday ☽

. . . .

9 Thursday

. . . .

Friday 10

Saturday 11

Sunday 12

This week's angel colour is **AMBER** –
appreciate your own good qualities.

Your spirit animal is the **MOUSE** –
pay attention to the details.

JULY *Week 29*

13 Monday

14 Tuesday

15 Wednesday

16 Thursday ●

Friday 17

Saturday 18

Ask your angels to help you balance your
karmic path by remembering past lives.

Sunday 19

This week's angel colour is **RUSSET** – a hug from
your angel will always make you feel warm and cosy.

Your spirit animal is the **TIGER** – nurture
your sense of adventure and be bold.

JULY *Week 30*

....

20 Monday

....

21 Tuesday

....

22 Wednesday

Ask your angel to make your life fascinating so
that you focus on every moment of every day.
....

23 Thursday

....

◑ Friday 24

Saturday 25

Sunday 26

This week's angel colour is **APRICOT** –
find time for thoughtful contemplation.

Your spirit animal is the **JACKAL** – take pleasure
in, and live within, every moment of every hour.

JULY *Week 31*

. . . .

27 Monday

Ask your angel to make you more optimistic
and adaptable so life doesn't shock you.
. . . .

28 Tuesday

. . . .

29 Wednesday

. . . .

30 Thursday

. . . .

○ Friday **31**

Saturday **1**

Pagan Festival of Lughnasdh: also known as Lammas
Eve and marks the first harvest of the year.

Sunday **2**

This week's angel colour is **TURQUOISE**
– be honest, even if it scares you.

Your spirit animal is the **RABBIT**
take a leap of faith.

August
Accept Your Gifts

It's very easy to think that something we're good at is easy, and that everyone can do it, but that isn't the case. This is a very big thing I've learned. So, take some time to sit and think about your gifts. It might even help to write a list. Make sure you include even the small things, like 'I'm easy to talk to,' because having someone who can listen makes a huge difference to many people. Some people are good at one big, noticeable thing, and others are good at several 'small' things. In either case, try to start each day with gratitude for your gifts, because that creates wonderful, angelic energy, which will in turn lead to wonderful events and experiences.

'I'm a wondrous and special being, and although I can't change the whole world, I can change the world for one person at a time.'

Marion's True Angel Story

My friend Sandra and I were always talking about angels, and she encouraged me to believe. I'm not sure I would have if it weren't for her. There are lots of things that wouldn't have been so good in my life without her. One thing she helped me with was confidence. In my family, all four of my siblings were very intelligent, got great grades and went on to have top careers. In contrast, I was a bit of a stay-at-home, I never got good grades and wouldn't have wanted to go to university anyway. Don't get me wrong – my parents loved me and never made me feel bad; I did that all by myself.

It took many years and lots of chats with Sandra before I realized that I was an important, maybe even vital, member of my family. Because with the best will in the world, my siblings were a little bit self-obsessed – they needed someone they could talk to, someone who wouldn't immediately turn the conversation around to their own problems, and that person was me.

In 2012, Sandra was killed in a car crash. I saw her in hospital just before she died, and she asked me to promise that

I wouldn't give up on angels. She told me that somehow she'd get her angel to send me a sign. Days later I was looking out of the window, thinking about Sandra and how she encouraged me to appreciate my talents. Suddenly I saw a large, pure white feather drift down onto the grass, and I thought, that's great, hun, but it's not really proof is it? *I mean, there are always feathers floating around. Then the feather started to move, and in the sunlight it gleamed different colours – pink, lilac, blue – as it twisted and turned. Then it just stopped in mid-air, turned until it was pointing at the window and then literally shot forwards and hit the glass right in front of my nose. It stuck there, slowly spinning on the spot until I had to admit it was no ordinary feather. Up close it sparkled as though it had been dusted in glitter, as though Sandra was saying, 'Tell me which bird this came from then!' I rushed outside to grab the feather, but when I reached the window it was gone. I searched everywhere, determined to find it, and even spent some time looking over fences to see if it had blown next door or into the road, but it had completely vanished. Even so, I know it was sent from Sandra's angel.*

It almost seems that Marion got this feather as a reward for following her friend's advice, not only to believe in angels, but also to accept the value of her natural gifts! We underestimate our own value all the time, and it's a pity we don't tell others how important they are to us more often. We all have gifts, every single one of us.

Kim's True Animal Angel Story

Our elderly dog, Juno, was usually very polite and well behaved. She was partially deaf and had poor sight, but we were still very close. She would always know if I was feeling down and take action to cheer me up, mostly by acting the fool with a big soppy grin on her face and her ears flapping around. One time she sensed that something was wrong with me before I even knew myself.

One day Juno started being very intrusive with her nose – rubbing it down one side of my tummy, and then trying to sniff my crotch. Naturally I told her to stop and even got quite cross, as she was so persistent it got embarrassing. I kept pushing her away, but she was quite insistent. In the middle of that night I had terrible stomach pains and Juno started going bonkers. It crossed my mind then that she'd been trying to tell me something with her 'inappropriate' attention. Normally I might have ignored my symptoms, thinking it was just a bug and would pass, but because of Juno I decided to go to hospital. The doctors quickly discovered that my appendix was about to rupture, and they operated immediately. As I recovered, my 'clown' kept me amused with her antics, and every time I looked into her eyes I knew that she was much more than 'just a dog'. If I hadn't gone to hospital right away, who knows what might have happened? I believe I owe Juno, who is my angel, my life.

This story shows the bond that exists between pets and their owners, as well as the empathy they have for us. It also tells us that deafness or any other ailment doesn't mean your pet is any less communicative than a 'perfect' one would be.

Facebook friends and their angels

Su Johnstone says:

'I was saved from drowning by an angel when I was nine years old, and I've felt them around me ever since, especially when I suffered badly from postnatal depression. I ask the angels for guidance and support at the beginning of every day, and thank them each evening before I go to sleep.'

....

○ Friday 31

....

Saturday 1

Pagan Festival of Lughnasdh: also known as Lammas
Eve and marks the first harvest of the year.
....

Sunday 2

....

This week's angel colour is **TURQUOISE**
– be honest, even if it scares you.

Your spirit animal is the **RABBIT**
– take a leap of faith.

AUGUST *Week 32*

....

3 Monday

....

4 Tuesday

♥ Ask your angel to bring you clear messages
and answers in your dreams.
....

5 Wednesday

....

6 Thursday

....

Friday 7

Saturday 8

Sunday 9

This week's angel colour is **BURGUNDY** – it's time to bring out your hidden reserves of energy!

Your spirit animal is the **GUINEA PIG** – seek out like-minded people and let them help you.

AUGUST *Week 33*

10 Monday

Ask your angel to improve your communication skills and thereby create new chances for you.

11 Tuesday

12 Wednesday

13 Thursday

● Friday 14

Saturday 15

Sunday 16

This week's angel colour is **PRIMROSE** – be softer this week, and trust in people.

Your spirit animal is the **MOLE** – be alert or you might miss a small miracle.

AUGUST *Week 34*

....

17 Monday

....

18 Tuesday

....

19 Wednesday

....

20 Thursday

....

Friday 21

● Saturday 22

Ask your angels to help you express
your wishes and hopes more clearly.

Sunday 23

This week's angel colour is **CARAMEL**
– is it time for a change of career?

Your spirit animal is the **BEAVER** – if you want to
be creative, think laterally to find a new direction.

AUGUST *Week 35*

....

24 Monday

....

25 Tuesday

....

26 Wednesday

Ask your angel to make you strong and independent, which will help you to find and keep true love.
....

27 Thursday

....

Friday 28

○ Saturday 29

Sunday 30

This week's angel colour is **MAGENTA** – feel
love for the universe and you'll get love back.

Your spirit animal is the **WOLF** – new knowledge
refreshes, so learn something different this week.

AUGUST/SEPTEMBER *Week 36*

31 Monday

....

1 Tuesday

Ask your angel to help you express yourself
through art, dance, song or writing.

....

2 Wednesday

....

3 Thursday

....

~~~~~

September
Enjoy Your Successes

~~~~~

*It's perfectly alright to be proud of your
achievements, as long as you don't make other
people feel inadequate in the process. This can
be tricky, because some people are very easily put
down and also sensitive to the successes of others.
So accept that you had a lot of help to get where
you are today, but also that you've worked very
hard. If someone looks a little envious when you
tell them about something you've done, ask if they
have a dream, and encourage them to believe in it.
Don't be afraid to admit that you've been helped
by angels, because by doing so you might open that
person to faith, and help them change their lives.*

**'I have worked hard and done well in
my life, and I'm not afraid to admit
it, or to tell people that the angels
have helped me to get where I am.'**

My True Angel Story

I've slotted something of my own story in here, because
I am someone who owes a huge amount to angels:

*Nearly 20 years ago I was in a terrible state – depressed,
overweight and feeling helpless and hopeless, despite having
everything I'd always wanted. But of course I know now that
didn't mean I had everything I needed. I had a wonderful
husband, son and home, and we had horses and dogs. I was
'living the life'. But despite all this, I was spiritually empty
inside. This gaping chasm was caused by my lack of belief
in anything specific. I'd been raised as a Catholic, but had
become disenchanted and left the faith when I was 19 years
old. This meant that by then, years later, the emptiness in my
soul was taking me over.*

*It was at my lowest point, when my mind had become
blank and receptive, that an angel spoke to me for the first
time. From that moment a series of miraculous events saw me
develop an unshakeable belief in reincarnation, write my first
book (I've now published 25!), write award-winning lyrics,*

host my own TV show, write magazine columns and articles, lose weight, meet someone I'd loved and lost in a past life, conquer a fear of flying and regenerate my love of life. I was lucky in some ways that my angel actually spoke to me, or I might never have had the courage to leap, but my husband and son came home that first day to find a new person, or rather a better version of my old self. I was back, stronger and more determined than ever.

Since that day I've done my absolute best to listen to every word, hear every signal and see every sign my angels have sent. Sometimes I've missed one or two, but always realized in the end. Believe me, no matter what state you're in, you can't be any worse than I was on that day, so stay faithful. I thank my angels every day for helping me make a success of my life, because without them I never would have got to where I am now. The talent they've given me to paint digital portraits of them enables me to show others their angel, which in turn helps them make the leap too. Today, after publishing 25 books, I sometimes look back on the person I used to be and marvel all over again at how angels helped me to transform my life.

Jay's True Angel Story

I was going to be late home and would be grounded for life! I'd come back to the car park and found it locked with my car inside. There was no way could I walk five miles home in my high heels. Mum had only allowed me to go out if I'd agree to be back by 11 p.m. It was now past then and I was stuck.

Then I saw something that really scared me. In the shadows, a man wearing a trench coat and a hat was getting out of a car. He came over to me and I shook with fear. I couldn't see his face, just the glitter of eyes. Then, for some reason, a feeling of total peace came over me and I felt safe. He held up a gloved hand from which dangled a key. 'You get home to your momma now,' he said in a voice that was mellow and reassuring. 'She's going to call the police if you don't go right away.' I ran to the gate, opened it and drove out, with the man watching me go. When I got home and ran into the kitchen, Mum was just picking up the phone.

Getting home late might seem like a small thing to bring about angel intervention, but who knows what might have happened without this angel's help. This story reminds me of others I've heard involving a 'baby angel', so why wouldn't he help a young person too?

Jacky's True Animal Story

We had a pure white German Shepherd dog called Fella, who we got from the pound. For many years he was our friend, and our children loved it when they were ill, as he'd sleep on their beds and keep them warm with his thick, snowy coat. One night I had a very strange dream in which I was visited by a jet-black dog. I'd never had a black dog, but I thought I knew him. He stood on the other side of a river, wagging his tail at me. Eventually I realized he was just like Fella, only black.

Fella would always tell the family when one of us was about to arrive home – he just seemed to know. He had a long and happy life with us, and I forgot about the dream. Then, one day, something awful happened. Fella had become quite old by then and he didn't see or hear very well. A tradesman called and left the back gate open. I'll never forgive myself for not realizing sooner, and by the time I did, Fella had wandered off. We all went out looking for him, and it was my oldest son Jake who found him. The poor old boy had slipped into the nearby river and drowned. I was devastated, and poor Jake had to pull him out all alone. Fella was still breathing then, but Jake said he suddenly went all light in his arms, and he knew our dog had passed.

It took me over a year to feel better, and it was then that I remembered the dream with the black dog. I'd been toying with the idea of getting another dog, and recalling the dream helped me make up my mind. I didn't feel like I'd be betraying Fella, as I had a theory about that dream. I went back to the pound – the same one where we'd got Fella all those years ago – and there was a one-year-old, black German Shepherd who was looking for a home. I thought of my dream again, of *how the black version of Fella had stood on the other side of the river staring back at me, and suddenly I knew that he'd been telling me, in the dream, that he would come back, rise from the waters and reappear as a black version of himself.*

I have no doubt that our animals can come back to us. We never really lose them. I tell everyone who'll listen how my angels showed me that Fella would come back. Some people believe it and some don't, but I love it when I see a spark of light dawning in someone's eyes, and I know I've planted a seed.

What a beautiful story, and so true. I know many people whose pets have come back to them in a new body, me included. This story demonstrates too, that no matter what our successes or failures, our pets will never blame us. To err is human, and often, to forgive is animal.

Facebook friends and their angels

J.H. Weaver says:

'I feel angels around me practically all the time, sometimes in human form and definitely in canine form. It's their energy I feel most, as they always come with love.'

31 Monday

1 Tuesday

Ask your angel to help you express yourself
through art, dance, song or writing.

2 Wednesday

3 Thursday

Friday 4

◐ Saturday 5

Sunday 6

This week's angel colour is **CREAM** – have
a quiet calm week. You deserve it!

Your spirit animal is the **DOLPHIN** – past
lives hold the secret to success in this life.

SEPTEMBER *Week 37*

....

7 Monday

....

8 Tuesday

....

9 Wednesday

....

10 Thursday

Ask your angel to help you project a sunny,
easy-going nature that uplifts others.
....

Friday 11

Saturday 12

● Sunday 13

This week's angel colour is **MUSTARD** – be
aware that someone may be manipulating you.

Your spirit animal is the **FOX** – the power of good
observation will help you. Stop, look, and listen.

. . . .

14 Monday

. . . .

15 Tuesday

. . . .

16 Wednesday

. . . .

17 Thursday

. . . .

Friday 18

Ask your angel to help you not to be afraid
– to be a leader rather than a follower.

Saturday 19

Sunday 20

This week's angel colour is **JADE** – a time
for benevolence and generosity of spirit.

Your spirit animal is the **GORILLA** – genuine
strength is always gentle. It has no need of force.

SEPTEMBER *Week 39*

21 Monday ◗

22 Tuesday

23 Wednesday

Pagan Festival of Mabon – also known as the Autumn
Equinox and the time of the main harvest.

24 Thursday

Friday 25

Saturday 26

Ask your angel to make you aware that everything you put into your body should have a purpose.

Sunday 27

This week's angel colour is **COBALT BLUE** – your intuition may improve this week.

Your spirit animal is the **PANDA** – male and female: don't forget to respect both sides of yourself.

28 Monday ○

....

29 Tuesday

....

30 Wednesday

♥ Ask your angel to help you appreciate your life and
all you have in it, especially those who love you.

1 Thursday

....

≺⦿≻

October
Cut Out the Deadwood
– Say 'No!'

≺⦿≻

Nobody likes disappointing others, and yet we don't seem to mind disappointing ourselves. We find it hard to say 'no' to someone, especially if we want them to like us. Being a pushover doesn't actually make someone like us – it makes them like using us. So, this month ask your angel to make you remember this: never *argue your point if you have to say no. Just simply say, 'Sorry, I can't.' If the other person asks 'Why?' or says 'Oh but…', then again just repeat, 'I'm sorry, I can't.' The fact that you've said that should be enough, and the reason why is your business.*

'I have my own path to walk, and others don't have the right to knock me off course whenever they feel like it.'

Chrissie's True Angel Story

I didn't really believe in angels for most of my life. I think many people have the same experience – they don't believe until they become desperate enough. It happened to me one dark winter's night. My beloved mum had been rushed into hospital with a suspected heart attack. Once she was there things went from bad to worse with the doctors predicting a very bad outcome. Mum had passed into a coma and they told us to prepare for the worst. They didn't expect her to make it through the night, so we said our tearful farewells at her bedside, holding her hands and telling her we loved her.

My sister and I were given sofas to curl up on because there was no way we were going home and leaving Mum alone. I remember being glad that my sister seemed to have fallen asleep, so we didn't have to keep voicing our worst fears. Every time we did we both broke down at the thought of Mum not being there for us. In my heart I was thinking about how Christmas, which was fast approaching, was going to be so empty without our anchor, the hub of our world, being there. I know most people love their mothers, but ours had brought us up alone, with no help from our dad, and he hadn't been near us for years. If Mum went, then we felt half of our lives would go too.

As I sat there I started to think about praying, but to whom should I pray? I wasn't religious and didn't think God would even know who I was. Then I recalled Mum telling us a story about an angel who helped children. I couldn't remember his name, but I started to talk to him anyway. Weirdly, it gave me comfort, and I could feel what seemed to be warmth around me, wrapping me up somehow.

After a while a blue light seemed to be right in front of me, like a column; then it slowly resolved into a classic angel shape, complete with wings. It coalesced and I could see that it was cradling a figure in its arms. It was Mum. I gasped. Was it taking her to heaven? I went from a non-believer to a believer in an instant and broke down, begging the angel not to take her away. The being nodded his head, and I didn't know if that meant he would or he wouldn't. I reached out a hand, but the angel retreated from me. I sobbed.

The next thing I knew, it was morning. I woke my sister and we rushed to Mum's bedside. She had her eyes open, and we both fell to her side, crying tears of joy and surprise. To this day I truly believe that the angel left Mum with us that night because I asked him to.

Something similar happened to me when my dad died, only that time he was meant to go, to leave this world, which by then held nothing but suffering for him. I got huge comfort from seeing his spirit form leave his earthly body, and his physical form become translucent. There was no doubt that he wanted to go and was joyous at breaking the link with his body, so how could I really mourn for his happiness?

Barbara's True Animal Angel Story

I started to wonder what was going on when I saw the same homeless man in three different places. It wasn't that odd I suppose, because the homeless do travel around a lot, moving from spot to spot in the city, seeking out new people to give them cash, etc. I had seen this one many times before, as he was a regular visitor to our local streets. I did recall that in the past he'd had a dog with him. My husband had begged me to stop giving money to the homeless, as he was concerned that they might spend it on drink or drugs, or even turn nasty with me. I didn't want to stop entirely, so I came up with a compromise – I would buy them a sandwich. That way they didn't get cash, but I could make sure they got some food.

On this particular day I'd already bought the homeless man a sandwich, but the third time I saw him he'd upped the ante as far as I was concerned, because he had the dog with him. This dog had proper 'spaniel' eyes – they were so big and brown you'd have thought his owner had added eyeliner. He was irresistible. I stopped to pet him and he was very friendly. I turned back to the man thinking that as I'd seen him several times it would be okay to say something, but he was gone. I was staggered.

I spun round in a circle, checking out the whole square, but there was literally nowhere he could have gone. I looked down, and was a bit surprised that the dog was still there, almost expecting that he would have vanished into the ether too. My hand was still on his head and he looked up at me trustingly. Needless to say, 'Tramp', as I came to call him, came to live with us and was a faithful companion, enhancing our lives for 10 years. I never saw that homeless man again, but I did hear that he'd died a day before he brought me his dog to look after.

Angels come in many guises. Was this the spirit of the homeless man, come back to bring his dog to someone he knew would care for it, or was he an angel bringing Barbara a friend she needed? Either way, I found the story magical.

Facebook friends and their angels

Ruthie Young says:

'I have absolute confidence that angels are there for me, and I'm very grateful. One time I was driving home in the middle of a really bad storm, trying to watch the road through the

pouring rain, when I heard someone say, 'Look UP! LOOK UP!' I did, and saw a tree just starting to topple. It fell across two lanes, and as I braked I skidded right up to the limbs of the tree, which were still waving from the fall. I would have surely been squashed if not for the warning, which must have come from my angel.'

SEPTEMBER/OCTOBER *Week 40*

28 Monday ○

29 Tuesday

30 Wednesday

Ask your angel to help you appreciate your life and all you have in it, especially those who love you.

1 Thursday

Friday 2

Saturday 3

◑ Sunday 4

This week's angel colour is **SILVER GREY** – try a new form of contemplation, such as yoga or reiki.

Your spirit animal is the **CHICKEN** – dig deep into your emotions and find their real causes.

OCTOBER *Week 41*

....

5 Monday

Ask your angel to help you be generous, but
also to know how and when to say 'no'.
....

6 Tuesday

....

7 Wednesday

....

8 Thursday

....

Friday **9**

Saturday **10**

Sunday **11**

This week's angel colour is **GINGER** – time for
some clutter clearing, both of mind and possessions.

Your spirit animal is the **LLAMA** – relax
and allow your angels to guide you.

OCTOBER *Week 42*

12 Monday

. . . .

13 Tuesday ●

. . . .

14 Wednesday

. . . .

15 Thursday

. . . .

Friday 16

Saturday 17

Ask your angel to help you let go of any
jealousy or emotional insecurity.

Sunday 18

This week's angel colour is **AZURE** – have a
personal conversation you've been avoiding.

Your spirit animal is the **SQUIRREL** – see
arguments from all sides, and find balance for all.

OCTOBER *Week 43*

. . . .

19 Monday

Ask your angel to increase your stamina and
strength so that you can pursue all you want to do.

. . . .

20 Tuesday ◑

. . . .

21 Wednesday

. . . .

22 Thursday

. . . .

Friday 23

Saturday 24

Sunday 25

This week's angel colour is **MAGNOLIA** – this might be a good time to fade into the background.

Your spirit animal is the **LEOPARD** – keep silent and allow your intuition to work on past lives.

....

26 Monday

....

27 Tuesday ○

....

28 Wednesday

....

29 Thursday

 Ask your angel to help you have the confidence to reach out and stretch yourself in new directions.

....

Friday 30

Saturday 31

Pagan Festival of Samhain: the time when the veil between the living and those who have passed away is at its thinnest.

Sunday 1

This week's angel colour is **CHOCOLATE** – this week will be rich and satisfying for you.

Your spirit animal is the **OTTER** – allow time for play and freedom.

November
Ask for Help if You Need It

The reverse side of the coin from last month is not to be afraid to ask for help if you need it. If you're lacking in confidence you might see others get help, but won't ask for it yourself!

Well, in fact, you will get help, maybe from your angel, or maybe from an earth-angel, but in order to get help you have to ask for it. Angels, like people, don't like to push their help on you, and need to be asked. And by allowing them to help you, you're actually honouring them. Talk to your angel or your friends. Be honest, say what you need and then trust that help will find its way to you.

'I am worthy of being helped, and I only need to ask.'

Sarah's True Angel Story

Three years ago I met a wonderful man called Jouni. At that time I'd lost my way a little and was quite negative about things, especially spiritual things. One day, out the blue, Jouni asked me about dreams and their interpretation, which led to lengthy and deep conversations about all things spiritual. The questions he asked prompted me to dig deep and tell him what I believed in. It felt like he was helping me to find myself again, and to restore my faith.

The best part came when we both had the exact same dream on the same night. We were astonished to say the least! I had never heard of that happening before and contacted a few psychics, who all said that Jouni and I are Twin Souls. I wasn't 100% sure, but we do share many of the signs, such as meeting by chance, the distance between us (I'm in Scotland, Jouni's in Finland) the age gap (he's 13 years younger than me), and other coincidences.

When a psychic told me that Jouni and I had talked in the in-between lives about how and when we would meet in the next life, I often wonder if I spoke to him about coming to find me if life was too tough. I know that sounds bizarre, but deep down inside it just felt like too much of a coincidence that he had entered my life at the time I needed him most. And since we found each other, the number of coincidences and synchronicities has been amazing.

One night Jouni asked if he could send me a Finnish song that he liked. It was called Minä ja Hän, which translates to 'Me and Him'. There was one line in the song that stood out: 'Mä tunnistan hänet rakkaakseni vaikka silmäni ummistan Se tahto on Herran' which translates as, 'I'll recognize him to be my true love, even with my eyes closed. It is God's will.' I took that as a sign that Jouni and I were Soul Mates.

Sarah is right. She gives beautiful examples of how, once we start accepting messages from angels, we get more and more of them. She can walk confidently towards the future, armed with this wonderful knowledge.

Caroline's True Animal Angel Story

A couple of years ago I had a hysterectomy, and afterwards was given clear instructions to take it easy and avoid lifting anything. My beautiful dog, Megan, never left my side as I lay in bed for the first week. She was my confidante and best friend. Being a person who loved the outdoors, I decided to go for small walks each day and take Megan with me. She had always been walked on the lead, but the strain of any pulling would be a problem for me. Something told me that Megan understood my situation, and I was right. Each day she would trot slowly by my side, and sit patiently while I took a little break. And each day we'd find a white feather at some point while out on our adventures.

Eventually I built up enough strength to make it as far as the local park. It was a beautiful time of the year and I remember seeing the green grass covered with white feathers, which was breathtaking. Most of our walks involved me sitting on a bench while Megan sat underneath, as we watched the world go by. This little ritual of ours carried on for eight weeks, and it was the first time I'd been able to share so much time with her. She was my shadow, my friend.

As my strength improved I noticed that Megan's had started to deteriorate, so I took her to the vet. I was given the heartbreaking news that she had a tumour and was very poorly. Following that diagnosis her health deteriorated very quickly. It was if she had held on for me and wanted to know that I was okay. The decision to have her put to sleep was the hardest one I've ever had to make.

I drove Megan to the vet, and as we entered a white feather fell from the sky in front of us. I sat with her for a long time before the vet gave her the injection. As the time had come to let her go and her life faded, I felt her soul leave her body. It was the most profound thing I've ever experienced. I'll never forget that day, and am so grateful that the angels were able to comfort me and wrap me in their wings as she passed over the rainbow bridge.

This story demonstrates both how angels will send us help from unexpected sources, and how our pets are so much more than just animals. This dog obviously delayed her rightful time to pass in order to help her mistress through a tough time. I've heard so many stories of how selfless animals can be, and how they will put their own suffering aside to help someone they love. The world would be a better place if we all took a second look at animals and their place in our world.

Facebook friends and their angels

Katie Jayne Dickinson says:

'I connect mainly with Archangels Michael, Raphael and Chamuel, and receive communication through clairsentience, visions, white feathers, music and the written word.'

Friday 30

Saturday 31

Pagan Festival of Samhain: the time when the veil between
the living and those who have passed away is at its thinnest.

Sunday 1

This week's angel colour is **CHOCOLATE** –
this week will be rich and satisfying for you.

Your spirit animal is the **OTTER** –
allow time for play and freedom.

NOVEMBER *Week 45*

. . . .

2 Monday

. . . .

3 Tuesday ◑

Ask your angel to help you enjoy life without unreasonable excesses that may harm you.

. . . .

4 Wednesday

. . . .

5 Thursday

. . . .

Friday 6

Saturday 7

Sunday 8

This week's angel colour is **CLARET** – don't
give up: what you seek is within your grasp.

Your spirit animal is the **BULL** –
creativity fills you with new ideas.

NOVEMBER *Week 46*

....

9 Monday

♥ Ask your angel to help you live in the moment,
so that you don't miss a second of your life.
....

10 Tuesday

....

11 Wednesday ●

....

12 Thursday

....

Friday 13

Saturday 14

Sunday 15

This week's angel colour is **PALE GREEN** – allow yourself to heal.

Your spirit animal is the **COYOTE** – you know the truth so reveal it without fear.

NOVEMBER *Week 47*

....

16 Monday

....

17 Tuesday

....

18 Wednesday

....

19 Thursday ◐

Friday 20

Saturday 21

Ask your angel to help you care for others
without ever being seen as 'interfering'.

Sunday 22

This week's angel colour is **FAWN** – your
problems are close to resolution, so relax.

Your spirit animal is the **BISON** – your
important possessions are in your heart.

NOVEMBER *Week 48*

. . . .

23 Monday

. . . .

24 Tuesday

. . . .

25 Wednesday ●

Ask your angel to help you find the right words
for any situation you find yourself in.
. . . .

26 Thursday

. . . .

Friday 27

Saturday 28

Sunday 29

This week's angel colour is **COPPER** – look deep within your soul to discover the real you.

Your spirit animal is the **KANGAROO** – keep moving forwards in leaps and bounds.

. . . .

30 Monday

. . . .

1 Tuesday

. . . .

2 Wednesday

Ask your angel to prepare you for a new year by
making a plan of what you want to achieve during it.

3 Thursday ☽

. . . .

December

Relish Thoughts of the Year Ahead

It's easy to be a little alarmed by an unknown future that might bring unsettling changes. We tend to feel more comfortable about a familiar situation, and even if we've settled into a bit of a rut and could do better, we still dread the unfamiliar. But we really don't need to feel fear. First, we must learn to enjoy living in the moment rather than in tomorrow, which doesn't yet exist. But, if we know that our angels are there for us, we can relish the future – be excited by it, relaxed in the knowledge that the more we believe in them the more likely it is that next year will bring better and more beautiful experiences than we had before.

'I trust in my angels implicitly, knowing that they will always do what's best for me.'

Virginia's True Angel Story

I've lived in West Virginia for most of my life. I was raised as a Catholic, but as a grown woman my spiritual beliefs have deepened. I believe in angels, and I believe that if one asks for the angels to assist them, they will. In my 55 years I've called upon them many times to protect my four children and me – they've always helped and so I have great faith in them.

My job as a radio DJ was the only one I'd had since college. We were often expected to make free appearances and take part in fundraisers when not on the air. This one Christmas season, I found myself in a trailer in the middle of a shopping centre parking lot, collecting canned food and money from listeners who dropped by. The charity we were helping out fed thousands of local families with food for Christmas. It was pretty much the end of the day and I was chatting with a co-worker named Gary, who was explaining that his and his wife's combined pay-cheques weren't enough to get their three children's toys and gifts out of layaway. They had two days until Christmas Eve, and no hope of getting the toys in time.

I watched Gary talking on the phone, telling his wife not to panic and that he would think of something. I immediately said to him 'Let's pray together, Gary, and ask God to send an Angel to help us.' We hadn't seen a person drive up to donate for a few minutes, so we just kept praying. I asked Gary how much money he needed and he told me it was $200. I said, 'Okay, if we're going to be visited by an angel, it had better be soon.'

We were about to clean up and go home for the evening when I opened the trailer door, and standing outside was the figure of a strange man. I couldn't believe my eyes, and I was stunned at the glow that seemed to emanate from his being. Before I could say anything, he handed me exactly $200 in cash and said, 'God wanted you to have this!' I glanced around to yell for Gary, and when I looked back the man/angel had vanished! There was no car or truck in sight, and nowhere he could have walked to within those couple of seconds! Gary hadn't seen a thing. I told him about the miracle and handed him the money, as it was clear the angel had brought it specifically for him, and we both cried as he phoned his wife to tell her. As soon as I regained my composure, I tried to describe what the angel had looked like, but I just couldn't. He was just a beautiful, glowing being with God's love pouring from his eyes.

To this day the experience has bonded Gary and me, and although we've since gone our separate ways, we'll always remember our angel visit at that charity radio broadcast. I believe that angels are just waiting to help us.

What a beautiful story for Christmas, and it should give us all hope and enthusiasm for 2016!

True Animal Angel Stories

I've changed things a little here, as it's Christmas, to bring a few true stories to your attention.

A 12-year-old Kenyan girl went missing from her home, and after a week of searching, her family feared the worst. She'd been kidnapped by a gang of men, one of whom wanted a wife, but was eventually found safe and sound, not in their hands, but surrounded by three lions. She said the lions had 'chased the bad men away' and then had remained with her, protecting her from all other wild predators. The lions would only leave when the police arrived to rescue her, as if they knew she would then be safe.

In Brookfield Zoo, Illinois, a three-year-old boy fell into the gorilla enclosure. This created a really dangerous situation because gorillas, like most captive animals, are very territorial and will rarely tolerate anyone entering their area uninvited. Gorillas are immensely strong, and even a young one would be impossible for an adult man to control if it got angry. The watching public, including the boy's parents, and the police and zookeepers barely dared move for fear of creating a violent reaction from the gorillas. However, a female gorilla called Binti picked up the boy and carried him gently to the enclosure door, where keepers were able to take him from her.

A similar thing happened at Jersey Zoo. A boy fell into the gorilla pit and lay unconscious until a silverback picked him up, cradled him in his arms and then placed him gently down and led the rest of the troop away so that the police could safely enter and retrieve him. Amazing photos of this event can be seen online.

When a woman called Joanne offered a home to Lu Lu, a potbellied pig, because no one wanted her and she was likely to end up slaughtered, she could not have known that this act of kindness would save her own life. Joanne had a heart attack in her back yard, all alone and with no one but Lu Lu to help her. It seems that Lu Lu first nudged her into a sitting position and then left the yard, made her way to a main road, and lay down there. Nobody stopped, and after a while the pig went back to check on her owner, who by then was conscious but unable to move or summon help. Lu Lu then went back to the road. Apparently, countless cars drove past the pig but didn't stop. Eventually someone did stop to see why the pig was lying in the road, instead of swerving around her as others had done. Lu Lu led the driver back to the yard and he was able to call paramedics, who saved Joanne's life.

I hope that stories such as these will fill you not only with the joy of the season, but hope and trust that members of the animal kingdom are making us change, albeit slowly, and will one day hold their righteous places in the world. We may be more 'intelligent' compared to animals when it comes to inventiveness and dexterity, but they are more spiritually aware than us, quite naturally, and have much to teach us.

Facebook friends and their angels

Mad Aunty says:

'I seem to talk to Michael and Raphael most of all. I ask Michael for protection and Raphael for help when I carry out reiki healing. I also ask them to heal other people I don't even know.'

....

30 Monday

....

1 Tuesday

....

2 Wednesday

Ask your angel to prepare you for a new year by
making a plan of what you want to achieve during it.
....

3 Thursday ◑

....

Friday 4

Saturday 5

Sunday 6

This week's angel colour is **NAVY BLUE** – sometimes you have to be a grown-up!

Your spirit animal is the **BUTTERFLY** – you are becoming better and better every day.

DECEMBER *Week 50*

7 Monday

8 Tuesday

Ask your angels to surround you with love and
companionship, especially at this time of year.

9 Wednesday

10 Thursday

● Friday 11

Saturday 12

Sunday 13

This week's angel colour is **BUTTERCUP**
– no more delaying tactics.

Your spirit animal is the **DOVE** – peace,
harmony and friendship are coming your way.

DECEMBER *Week 51*

....

14 Monday

....

15 Tuesday

....

16 Wednesday

....

17 Thursday

....

Friday 18

Ask your angel to enable you to help others who have no love or companionship at this time of year.

Saturday 19

Sunday 20

This week's angel colour is **EMERALD GREEN** – you are as precious as a jewel.

Your spirit animal is the **FISH** – be close to the refreshing, revitalizing power of water this week.

DECEMBER *Week 52*

....

21 Monday

....

22 Tuesday

Pagan festival of Yule – Winter Solstice. The longest
night of the year, recognized as the start of winter.
....

23 Wednesday

....

24 Thursday – Christmas Eve

 Ask your angel to be open to what life
brings you in the next 12 months.
....

....

○ Friday – Christmas Day **25**

....

Saturday – Boxing Day **26**

....

Sunday **27**

....

This week's angel colour is **CARMINE** – it's time for change, so go for it!

Your spirit animal is the **PEACOCK** – be aware of your own natural beauty!

DECEMBER 2016 *Week 1*

28 Monday

29 Tuesday

♥ Ask your angel to make your dreams
come true in the year ahead.

30 Wednesday

31 Thursday

Friday 1

Saturday 2

Sunday 3

This week's angel colour is **HONEY** – things that generally annoy you will just pass you by.

Your spirit animal is the **TURTLE** – concentrate on walking a peaceful path.

JANUARY

M	T	W	T	F	S	S
				1	2	3
4	5	6	7	8	9	10
11	12	13	14	15	16	17
18	19	20	21	22	23	24
25	26	27	28	29	30	31

FEBRUARY

M	T	W	T	F	S	S
1	2	3	4	5	6	7
8	9	10	11	12	13	14
15	16	17	18	19	20	21
22	23	24	25	26	27	28
29						

MARCH

M	T	W	T	F	S	S
	1	2	3	4	5	6
7	8	9	10	11	12	13
14	15	16	17	18	19	20
21	22	23	24	25	26	27
28	29	30	31			

APRIL

M	T	W	T	F	S	S
				1	2	3
4	5	6	7	8	9	10
11	12	13	14	15	16	17
18	19	20	21	22	23	24
25	26	27	28	29	30	

MAY

M	T	W	T	F	S	S
30	31					1
2	3	4	5	6	7	8
9	10	11	12	13	14	15
16	17	18	19	20	21	22
23	24	25	26	27	28	29

JUNE

M	T	W	T	F	S	S
		1	2	3	4	5
6	7	8	9	10	11	12
13	14	15	16	17	18	19
20	21	22	23	24	25	26
27	28	29	30			

JULY

M	T	W	T	F	S	S
				1	2	3
4	5	6	7	8	9	10
11	12	13	14	15	16	17
18	19	20	21	22	23	24
25	26	27	28	29	30	31

AUGUST

M	T	W	T	F	S	S
1	2	3	4	5	6	7
8	9	10	11	12	13	14
15	16	17	18	19	20	21
22	23	24	25	26	27	28
29	30	31				

SEPTEMBER

M	T	W	T	F	S	S
			1	2	3	4
5	6	7	8	9	10	11
12	13	14	15	16	17	18
19	20	21	22	23	24	25
26	27	28	29	30		

OCTOBER

M	T	W	T	F	S	S
31					1	2
3	4	5	6	7	8	9
10	11	12	13	14	15	16
17	18	19	20	21	22	23
24	25	26	27	28	29	30

NOVEMBER

M	T	W	T	F	S	S
	1	2	3	4	5	6
7	8	9	10	11	12	13
14	15	16	17	18	19	20
21	22	23	24	25	26	27
28	29	30				

DECEMBER

M	T	W	T	F	S	S
			1	2	3	4
5	6	7	8	9	10	11
12	13	14	15	16	17	18
19	20	21	22	23	24	25
26	27	28	29	30	31	

Useful Contacts

Name:

Phone:

Email:

....

Name:

Phone:

Email:

....

Name:

Phone:

Email:

....

Name:

Phone:

Email:

....

Name:

Phone:

Email:

....

Name:

Phone:

Email:

....

Name:

Phone:

Email:

....

Name:

Phone:

Email:

....

Name:

Phone

Email:

....

Name:

Phone:

Email:

....

Name:

Phone:

Email:

....

Name:

Phone:

Email:

....

Name:

Phone:

Email:

....

Name:

Phone

Email:

....

Name:

Phone:

Email:

....

Reminders

Resources

SCIENTIFIC ARTICLES

How mindfulness meditation can improve decision-making:
www.sciencedaily.com/releases/2014/02/140212112745.htm

How regular spiritual practice may help to guard against depression:
www.sciencedaily.com/releases/2014/01/140116084846.htm

How many people who have had strong spiritual experiences encounter a perception of oneness:
www.bibliotecapleyades.net/ciencia/ciencia_holouniverse05.htm

Is science proving the existence of a spiritual realm?
www.examiner.com/article/is-science-proving-god-exists

OTHERS

Name meanings: www.behindthename.com

Colour meanings:
www.universeofsymbolism.com/color-meaning.html

Meanings of smells: www.thequickenedword.com/rhema/OpenedSmellAromasList.htm

Meaning of metals:
www.thewhitegoddess.co.uk/the_elements/the_metals.asp

Therapies to help your pets:
www.emotionalhealing4animals.co.uk

Join the
HAY HOUSE
Family

As the leading self-help, mind, body and spirit publisher in the UK, we'd like to welcome you to our community so that you can keep updated with the latest news, including new releases, exclusive offers, author events and more.

Sign up at www.hayhouse.co.uk/register

Like us on Facebook at Hay House UK

Follow us on Twitter @HayHouseUK

www.hayhouse.co.uk

 Hay House Publishers
Astley House, 33 Notting Hill Gate, London W11 3JQ
020 3675 2450   info@hayhouse.co.uk

ABOUT THE AUTHOR

Tony Smedley

Jenny Smedley has had a strong connection with angels since she was a small child. Her earliest memory comes from when she was just three years old: thinking she was being separated from her mum, she jumped from a moving train and was snatched to safety by a pair of mysterious, unseen arms.

Now based in the beautiful county of Norfolk, and happily married for over 40 years, Jenny Smedley DPLT is a qualified past-life regressionist, author, TV and radio presenter and guest, international columnist and spiritual consultant, specializing in angels and past lives. She lives with her husband, Tony, a spiritual healer, and her reincarnated 'Springador' dog, KC.

For two years she hosted her own spiritual chat show on Taunton TV, interviewing people such as David Icke, Reg Presley, Uri Geller and Diana Cooper. Jenny has appeared on many TV shows in the UK, the USA, Ireland and Australia, including *The Big Breakfast*, *Kelly*, *Open House*, *The Heaven and Earth Show*, *Kilroy* and *Jane Goldman Investigates*, as well as hundreds of radio shows, including *The Steve Wright Show* on BBC Radio 2, and *The Richard Bacon Show* on Five Live in the UK, and many in the USA, Australasia, South Africa and Spain. She is currently a columnist for *Chat – it's fate* and *Soul & Spirit* in the UK, *Take 5* in Australia and *Lucky Break* in New Zealand, where she also creates digital portraits of readers' angels.

www.jennysmedley.com